What Christian Leaders Have Said about Ron Dunn's Teaching

I have read scores of books about evil in the world and suffering in the lives of Christians—and have even written a book on the topic myself—but this one is outstanding. Ron Dunn is not afraid to face facts honestly, nor is he inexperienced in applying God's truth lovingly. He himself has been in the furnace and found Jesus there with him, so pay attention to what he says.

—Warren W. Wiersbe,
author of the "BE" series of Bible Studies

There was a day when I measured all excellence in biblical exegesis by Ron Dunn's pulpit insight. I was a pastor then. But in the intervening years since I've been teaching, I realize that here and there in the homiletic world there comes a man whom the young preachers must read and the old ones must remember, if ever we hope to keep the Bible central in our pulpit and lives. Ron Dunn was such a man. He made God's truth accessible, and even now as he enjoys heaven, we who still live in what C. S. Lewis called "the Shadowlands" can be grateful that his words are still being published and can continue to live on for those who were denied his insights while he lived and preached among us.

—Calvin Miller, best-selling author

Ron Dunn is in a class by himself. I know of no preaching anywhere that stimulates me or encourages me like that of Ron Dunn. His messages are fresh, stimulating, and uniquely original. I prophesy that his impact will be legendary.

—Adrian Rogers, former pastor, Bellevue Baptist Church

Of all the preachers I heard over the years in conferences, Ron Dunn is my favorite. Get his books, listen to his CDs and DVDs every chance you get. God will speak to you through this mighty man of God.

—Jimmy Draper, former president,
LifeWay Christian Resources

Over the years, one has come to expect wisdom, balance, and insight from Ron Dunn. It should be no surprise that Dr. Dunn, in *Will God Heal Me?* brings all three in great abundance to the "signs and wonders" controversy. So much is being taught and said today that will ultimately hurt rather than heal God's people. This book will give you the truth . . . the biblical truth from a man who knows the Bible, knows the God who gave us the Bible, and knows for and cares for the people for whom it is written. In a fallen world where there is pain, suffering, and unanswered prayers, this book is a must read. If you read no other on the subject, read it. You'll be glad you did.

—Steve Brown, professor of Practical Theology, Reformed
Theological Seminary, Orlando, Florida
President and Bible Teacher,
Key Life Network, Inc., Maitland, Florida

Ron Dunn's book *Will God Heal Me?* is a good example of devotional and theological honesty written from a deep reservoir of scriptural study, pastoral perspective, and from his own personal experiences with grief. Ron Dunn has written a book that combines biblical insight with honest human emotion. I highly recommend *Will God Heal Me?* to anyone who grapples with questions of pain and suffering and, indeed, to anyone who either personally or on behalf of another struggles with the experiences of suffering.

—Robert B. Sloan Jr., president,
Baylor University, Waco, Texas

Ron Dunn writes with an authenticity which comes through experience and authority borne out of sound biblical scholarship. His transparency brings a fresh approach to the timeless question: *Will God Heal Me?* This is a book you will read and return to time and again. Don't be surprised if you often find yourself quoting from this highly respected author and Bible teacher.

—Thomas D. Elliff, pastor,
First Southern Baptist Church, Del City, Oklahoma

will *God*

heal me?

Foreword by Michael Catt

will God

heal me?

God's Power and Purpose in Suffering

RON DUNN

B&H
PUBLISHING GROUP

Nashville, Tennessee

978-1-4336-8037-3

Published by B&H Publishing Group

Nashville, Tennessee

Dewey Decimal Classification: 231.8

Subject Heading: SUFFERING \ GOD \ CHRISTIAN LIFE

Unless otherwise indicated, all Scripture quotations are taken from the *New American Standard Bible,* © Copyright 1960, 1995, by The Lockman Foundation. Used by permission.

Scripture quotations marked NKJV, are taken from the *New King James Version,* Copyright © 1982 by Thomas Nelson, Inc. Used by permission. All rights reserved.

Scripture quotations marked KJV are taken from the *King James Version* of the Bible.

1 2 3 4 5 6 7 8 • 17 16 15 14 13

To a wonderful mother-in-law
EILEENE COOK MITCHELL
Who loves me no matter what I write

Contents

Acknowledgments xv

Foreword by Michael Catt xvii

Introduction: There's a New God in Town 1

Part One
When Illness Strikes

1. When Questions Come 9
   Why Doesn't God Just Release His Power and Heal All the Hurts?

2. The Night Side of Life 15
   The Losses and Gains of Suffering

3. Where Does Sickness Come From? 31
   Is God in Sovereign Control of His Universe?

4. By the Rivers of Babylon 42
   The Modern-Day Stigmas of Sickness

5. The Seduction of the Sick 56
   Have We Embraced a Pagan Value?

6. The Seducers 63
   All Seduction Is in Fact Self-Seduction

Part Two
Handling Accurately the Word of Truth

7. What Do We Mean by "Healing"?   75
   An Important Definition of Terms

8. Handling Accurately the Word of Truth   81
   Careful, Thorough Bible Study Is Vital to a Faith
   That Truly Honors God

9. Cutting It Straight: Part One   86
   Understanding Three Essential Rules of Biblical
   Interpretation

10. Cutting It Straight: Part Two   100
    How to Correctly Interpret a Specific Bible Passage

11. Healing: The Same Yesterday, Today, and Forever?   111
    Are the Miracles of the New Testament Being
    Repeated Today?

12. The Healings of Jesus and the Apostles: A Closer Look   122
    Are They Valid Models for Modern-Day Healing?

13. Did Christ Die to Make Us Healthy?   139
    Do You Have the Right to Be Healed?

14. Does God Always Want Us Well?   146
    The Harmful Side Effects of Unscriptural Teaching

Part Three
Finding God's Good in Suffering

15. Divine Temple or Clay Pot?   157
    Christians Experience Pain Like Everyone Else but
    with One Redeeming Difference

16. Praying for the Sick   166
    What You Do Not Receive, You Do Not Require

17. When God Says No   180
    God Often Draws Outside the Lines We Have Drawn
    for Him

18. "I've Come to Help You Die"   194
    There Are No Cures, Only Postponements

19. Something Better than Healing   204
    The "God-Ultimate Purpose" of Suffering

20. Fear Not   214
    We Can Have Joy in the Presence of Heartache

Part Four
Resources

Notes   225

About the Author   233

Acknowledgments

It's been said that no one writes a book alone. Never has that been more true of a book than of this one. My heartfelt gratitude to:

- Dan Benson, my editor, who knows just what to say when the going is rough.
- Dr. Robert Sloan, president of Baylor University, who read big chunks of the manuscript and made invaluable suggestions.
- Dr. Ron Hardin of Little Rock, Arkansas, who read every part of the manuscript dealing with medical issues and, even up to the last minute, made valuable contributions.
- Les Stobbe, for his editorial counsel and input, and Lisa Lauffer, for her capable assistance with the final edit.
- Joanne Gardner, my assistant for thirty years, who is a vital part of every book I write.
- Stephen M. Dunn, my son, whose expertise with my computer and its stubborn ways helped keep me sane and who spent long hours typing and formatting the manuscript. I certainly could not have done it without his help.
- The precious people who unselfishly shared their experiences of illness to make this book possible.

- My wife, Kaye, who not only did her share of typing, but read my pages with a close and constructive eye and offered great suggestions, which make this a better book than it would have been otherwise. The smartest thing I ever did was to marry this girl.

Foreword

One of the hardest days of my life was the day I got the call that Ron Dunn had breathed his last and entered into his reward. I was happy for him, but honestly I was selfish. There was more I wanted to say to him. There were more sermons I wanted him to preach. There were more books for him to write to edify the saints. But God had other plans.

When Ron wrote *Will God Heal Me?* he did not take the popular path. We had several one-on-one discussions about this book and how one publisher told him if he would "lighten it up a little" it would sell more. Ron was too committed to an accurate exegesis of Scripture to worry about sales. While others were proclaiming a health-and-wealth theology, Ron went deep in Scripture to see what God said about healing and miracles. Ron didn't write to make money; he wrote to speak truth into our lives.

Ron had his share of sickness and suffering. The last year of his life was difficult. He was bedridden with a hemorrhagic lung disease. The disease had been previously misdiagnosed. It was while he was preaching his last Bible conference at Sherwood that a doctor in our church discovered the real problem.

After preaching the morning service, we had to put Ron on oxygen and take him to the hospital. He had surgery here in

Albany and then had several weeks of recovery before he was well enough to travel home. Little did I know, it would be the last time he preached for me.

In the last few months of his life, Ron was working on a series of new messages from Paul's letter to the Philippians. I watched Ron live out Philippians 3:10: "that I may know Him, and the power of His resurrection, and the fellowship of His sufferings." It would be his last and lasting message.

His last Bible conference was at MacArthur Boulevard Baptist Church in Irving, Texas, where he pastored during days of great revival in the 1970s. Ron was dying, but we didn't know that at the time. Pastors and others around the country had been praying for his healing. We needed Ron, and we longed for God to extend his days.

During that conference, Ron preached out of Philippians. David Allen, the pastor of the church, said Philippians 3:10 was "autobiographical for Ron. During his lifetime, God had given him, not only to know about Christ, but to know him in an intimate way. He also knew of the power of his resurrection and the fellowship of his sufferings."

His last sermon was at First Southern Baptist Church in Del City, Oklahoma, where his long-time friend Tom Elliff was pastor. Somehow, Ron drove himself to Del City, preached that morning, and drove himself home. In just a short time, he was back in the hospital, and this time he wasn't going to check out.

Several pastors preached Ron's funeral. Tom Elliff and I had the privilege of being with the family for a private graveside service. After the funeral, I went back and looked at devotionals Ron had written during those last months. One was entitled "The God Who Is Present and the God Who Is Hidden," in which he wrote:

"Where can I go from Your Spirit? Or where
can I flee from Your presence? If I ascend to heaven,
You are there; if I make my bed in Sheol, behold,
You are there" (Psalm 139:7–8).

During the months (coming up on five) I have
been ill, about the only thing constructive, apart
from praying, I've been able to do is read. I found a
new joy in reading and studying the Bible, as well
as other things. One of the books that has been a
special blessing is St. Augustine's *Confessions*. . . .
In Part 4 of Book One, these words captured my
attention: "You are the most hidden from us and
yet the most present amongst us." Present yet
hidden—what an apt description of our God. At
least it was in my present situation. I knew that
God was present because the Bible said so and my
own experience echoed it. . . . What I want to say
is there are many times and situations in which it
looks as though God has abandoned us, or at least,
misplaced us. We have probably all felt this way. But
even though God may be visibly hidden from us,
we must remember that He is always present.

In another devotional, written just a few weeks before his
death, Ron unknowingly captured the essence of the book you
hold in your hands. He wrote another devotional based on
Philippians 3:10 titled "That I May Know Him."

As many of you know, I have been ill for the
past seven months and haven't preached since
September. I lay in the hospital for six weeks, then
spent an additional six months at home in bed. At
the same time my daughter Kimberly was in a car

wreck in November and, because of severe infec-
tions, had to have her left foot amputated a couple
of weeks ago.

Recently Kaye was diagnosed with lymphomic
cancer and is undergoing chemotherapy. While I
was lying helpless in the hospital with lung disease,
I thought I was going to die, then, in bed helpless
at home, I thought I was going to be an invalid; it
looked as though my preaching days might be over.
I know now that I will preach again (starting May
13th), but the doctor tells me I will never recover
my full lung capacity and will not be able to pursue
my ministry as aggressively as before.

But before I knew that, I lay in bed thinking,
"Of what value am I now?" Everything that made
my life purposeful seemed to have been cannibal-
ized by my disease. During this time I was led
to start reading and studying Paul's letter to the
Philippians. God both rebuked me and encouraged
me. He said to me that there was more to being His
child than preaching, and if I found my worth only
in health and strength and preaching, I was missing
a big point.

The big point being that my ultimate aim in
life was none of these, but "THAT I MAY KNOW
HIM." In Philippians 3:10, Paul brings to a conclusion the story of his conversion and sets his goal. In
verses 7 and 8 he speaks of counting all his gains as
loss that he might gain Christ; gradually he leads up
to the ultimate goal. Read it like this:

IN ORDER THAT
I might gain Christ
and
be found in Him
having the righteousness that is from God
based on faith in Christ

SO THAT
I may know Him.

"That I may know Him." That I may know Him
more intimately, that my relationship with Him may
grow deeper and deeper, never ceasing nor slowing
this growth until I see Him in the final resurrection.

But that's not all the apostle says; he goes on
to describe what this deeper knowing of Christ
involves: "The power of His resurrection and the
fellowship of His sufferings." To know Christ means
to know the power of His resurrection and the fellowship of His sufferings.

Some observations: It is strange that he should
speak of power and sufferings in the same statement. We normally think power would cancel out
any sufferings, as I'm afraid many do. But Paul
asserts there is no inconsistency between the
power and the sufferings. Both are part of the same
experience.

Note the sequence: power, then sufferings. We
would probably have reversed the order: sufferings,
then power. And of course, with Christ that was the
order: He had to suffer before He knew the power
of the resurrection. For us it is the opposite—first

the power and then the sufferings. The power of the resurrection is the life-giving power of God, manifested in the raising of Christ from the dead, which also works in us (Ephesians 1:19). When we are saved, we experience the power, but then we experience the sufferings. It is the power of the resurrection than enables us to share in His sufferings.

That the "sufferings" were the ultimate experience is plain by its coming after the power of His resurrection, and that Paul further amplifies it with "being made conformable to His death." So the bottom line is that we are to share in His sufferings, enabled to do this by the power of His resurrection that resides in us. This is what it means to "know Him" in the way Paul meant.

To take as our ultimate aim in life "to know Him" is to have an aim and purpose that nothing can interfere with or take away. Stripped by sickness, affliction, or poverty or anything else cannot prevent us from coming to Him in a deeper and more intimate fashion.

You hold in your hands a treasure of truth. Read it carefully. Share it with a friend. You or someone you know will need this book in the coming days.

Ron is home and free of his disease; we are not home yet. But though he is dead, he still speaks.

Michael Catt
Sherwood Baptist Church
Albany, Georgia

There's a New God in Town

IT WAS BOUND TO HAPPEN.

I knew that sooner or later they would have to do something like this—and there is was in the paper: an article telling of a new pamphlet just released by the National Institute of Health titled *Everything Doesn't Cause Cancer.* In recent years, the report explained, so much has been said about cancer and its many causes, the United States was developing cancer-paranoia. It was time to set the record straight: Not everything causes cancer (nearly everything but not quite everything).

For me the report came just in time. I was beginning to develop my own little case of cancer-paranoia. Only a few days before, a local paper had carried this headline at the bottom of page one: "Studies Link Shampoo with Cancer." This was not welcome news to someone who is inclined toward clean hair. The article went on to report that laboratory mice had developed cancer after being fed shampoo for six months. Well, anybody who drinks shampoo for six months deserves whatever they get, whether cancer or split ends. But with headlines like that, it's no wonder we are afraid to touch, taste, or smell anything without the *Good Housekeeping* Seal of Approval or a sworn affidavit from the FDA guaranteeing its safety—and we're not sure about the FDA anymore either.

Have you ever asked yourself how this preoccupation with health started, why as Christians we are so afraid of ill health? When I was a child, no one I knew gave much thought to what we put into our bodies. We judged what was good to eat by its taste, not its content. For us, fried eggs, bacon dripping with fat, red meat, whole milk, and vegetables cooked in bacon grease and butter was down-home cooking at its best. I cannot remember anyone jogging unless they were going somewhere in a hurry. We had never heard of aerobics. DDT was the major weapon against insects, and asbestos was our armor against fire. Every man I knew smoked, plus a few scandalous women. Diet drinks and food supplements were not a part of our vocabulary. Seat belts belong in airplanes, helmets on race-car drivers.

Then came the 1960s. If you're old enough, you remember the Surgeon General's report on smoking. Suddenly people began to start thinking about health on a nationwide scale. Coca-Cola invented Tab, sugar substitutes appeared in every kitchen and restaurant, and we began measuring the sodium content of every morsel we ate. By the eighties new diet books were leaping to the top of the best-seller list. Today we are told that one out of every three Americans is currently on a diet, and that one in five adults participates in aerobic exercise. Fitness salons have sprung up in every neighborhood. I drove through a small town recently where the local barbershop boasted two tanning salons. The jogging trail across the street from our house needs a traffic cop.

I can't remember the last time I sat down at a meal without a health-conscious Pharisee measuring everything on my plate that was unhealthy. A little get-together with friends can be dangerous if you don't guard your tongue. At one recent gathering I recklessly mentioned that I didn't know my cholesterol level. Conversations halted in mid-sentence, mouths gaped, and eyes gawked. "You don't KNOW?" I felt I should cover my face in shame and repent in sackcloth and ashes. I now know my cholesterol level, and it's good.

Health Consciousness: Good for Business

And wouldn't you know it, health care and physical fitness have become big business. On billboards and TV, hospitals compete for business just like Coca-Cola and Pepsi compete for consumers. They merge to enhance the bottom line, not necessarily to improve care for patients or fitness-center customers. I have a 1-800 Dial-A-Doctor number. Good nutritional value is a major marketing tool. High fiber and low fat is the winning combination. Breakfast cereals now have an "honest, natural" taste, and even beer is less filling. I just returned from the vending machine in my hotel where I purchased a package of potato chips. Faced with several choices, I chose the one that advertised "Cholesterol-free, Low Saturated Fats."

To their credit, some churches have grafted health and fitness into their official ministry tree, offering Olympic-sized swimming pools and recreational programs for the whole family. I have seen "Jogging for Jesus" classes and "Slim for the Savior" diet seminars—the church seeking to minister to the body as well as to the spirit. Somewhere right now a church aerobic class is going through its drill accompanied by a jazzy rendition of "Love Lifted Me."

Before I sat down to write this morning, my wife and I walked three miles around the track, then drank some freshly squeezed orange juice. We will do another three miles this evening.

As a result of all this emphasis on health, Americans are living longer and healthier lives than any citizenship in modern history. In the second century after Christ, at the height of the Roman Empire, the average life expectancy was less than twenty-five years. Only four out of one hundred men lived beyond the age of *fifty*. For the Empire to maintain even a stationary population, every woman had to bear five children.[1]

Poking fun at our health consciousness is great sport. Yet no one in their right mind is against health and fitness. We do not honor God when we dishonor our bodies, for they are the temples of the Holy Spirit.

But there is another side to all this. Biologist Lewis Thomas makes the astonishing observation that, at a time when we should be celebrating our good shape, "we have just now become convinced of our bad health, our constant jeopardy of disease and death . . . rapidly becoming a nation of hypochondriacs, living gingerly, worrying ourselves half to death. . . . As a people we have become obsessed with health."[2]

A New God in Town

And so there is a new god in town. This new god is a two-headed one, Health and Fitness, the Bel and Nebo of our day (Isa. 46:1). The followers of this new god worship from dawn's early light to the fading shadows of evening, seven days a week, sometimes alone, often in small groups or large gatherings. They worship indoors and outdoors, on sidewalks and in parks, in homes and offices, in cold weather or hot. They are a determined congregation. This latest golden calf possesses cultic dimensions, eclipses denominational lines, spans the generation gap, and is oblivious to race, creed, or color.

You'll quickly recognize this god's truly devoted disciples. You may find them clad in designer jogging togs, color-coordinated leg warmers, and expensive running shoes—or eschewing fashion statements, they may simply dress in old gym shorts, ragged T-shirts, and dust-covered tennis shoes. Huffing and puffing through malls or in the streets, in sunshine, or rain, these most devoted worshippers fall before their god with sacrifices of sweat and sweets.

Again, this is all good for the body and great fun for the spirit. But what happens when sickness removes us from this scene, when suffering intrudes on our normal life? Of course, we're never really prepared for this. It catches us by surprise and knocks us off balance.

Fear Fuels Devotion to Health

One, if not the first, emotion we feel when illness intrudes is fear. It's not just fear of the illness itself, but fear of what it will do to our future, our plans, of where it may take us. And fear of how others may respond. Not even the church appears ready to respond, for few churches provide for the ill and suffering like they do for the healthy.

Underlying our fear of ill health is our insecurity about where God fits into the picture. Will God move upon my body to heal me? Or will I have to live with this? Or die with it? These are questions that I have faced, and perhaps you have too. In fact, you may be facing them right now.

As we address these tough questions, let's keep in mind Paul's magnificent words of hope. "Now to Him who is able to do far more abundantly beyond all that we ask or think, according to the power that works within us, to Him be the glory" (Eph. 3:20–21).

To God be the glory.

There may be more to suffering than the pain.

—Ron Dunn

PART ONE

When Illness Strikes

Being ill is just another way of living, but by the time we
have lived through illness we are living differently.
—Arthur Frank, *At the Will of the Body*

Religion is for people who are afraid to go to hell;
Spirituality is for people who have already been there.
—Martha Manning, *Undercurrents*

CHAPTER 1

When Questions Come

Why Doesn't God Just Release His Power and Heal All the Hurts?

"DOES GOD HEAL TODAY?" THE question is as relevant as your next headache. Even more relevant is "Will God heal *me*?"

It's easy to philosophize about suffering when you're not doing any. But when the beast crouches at your own door, it's another ball game—the answers don't come as easily then, and the explanations often don't satisfy.

C. S. Lewis spoke prophetically in the preface of *The Problem of Pain* when he said, "The purpose of the book is to solve the intellectual problem raised by suffering; for the far higher task of teaching fortitude and patience I was never fool enough to suppose myself qualified, nor have I anything to offer my readers except my conviction that when pain is to be borne, a little courage helps more than much knowledge, a little human sympathy more than much courage, and the least tincture of the love of God more than all."[1]

The Problem of Pain is one of the best books ever written on the subject. However, twenty years later when Lewis' wife lay dying of cancer, he found no comfort in the things he had written. The things he had written were no less true, but he was less able to affirm them.

When the daughter of a fellow pastor died suddenly of a rare disease, someone asked him if he still believed in Romans 8:28. Did he still believe that all things worked together for good for God's people?

"Yes, I still believe that," he said, "but don't ask me to preach on it just yet."

When things happen that make us look as though we no longer believe, the problem is not faith, but an inability to affirm it in the shroud of darkness. Like the father of the demon-possessed boy, we cry, "Lord, I believe; help thou mine unbelief!"

Sufferings to which we cannot resign ourselves produce within us a weariness that, as Kornelis Miskotte points out, "is not merely a manifestation of the exhaustion of creaturely life but also of a deterioration of the power of faith to affirm it."[2]

Sickness makes us do strange things. Actor Steve McQueen went to Mexico for laetrile treatments. Stricken by a rare form of large-cell carcinoma, comedian Andy Kaufman traveled to the Philippines to see a psychic healer. People searching for cures have tried everything from crystals to pyramids, megaherbs to psychic hotlines.

Pain can make us desperate. If we're not satisfied with conventional treatment, we may seek alternative treatments unendorsed by traditional medicine. Some alternatives may prove valid—even miraculous. Others may flirt with quackery, but at least they are something to do and try. We are not too proud to do anything. Satan told the truth when he said, "Skin for skin, yea, all that a man hath will he give for his life" (Job 2:4 KJV).

My Personal Search

I am not a hostile witness in the case of divine healing. This book is the result of my own personal search, a search that began when my faith suddenly collided with sickness, suffering, and death.

"Skin for skin," the Devil said. And it was my skin and the skin of my family. My supreme motivation was selfish. In spite of all my prayers and the concentrated prayers of my church, my mother died of cancer at the age of sixty. Despite the prayers of my wife and me, our church, and hundreds of friends across the country, our son was not healed of manic depression and committed suicide when he was eighteen. My father-in-law died of cancer when he was sixty-two, in spite of many prayers and claims of healing. In the early eighties I suffered some severe physical problems. From 1976 till 1986 I struggled with major depression and wasn't helped until I started seeing a psychiatrist.

Meanwhile, I was writing a book on the power of prayer and preaching around the world on the victorious Christian life. My life had become a paradox.

Someone said to me, "You don't have enough faith to be healed." But that was not my problem. My problem was I didn't have enough faith to stay sick, if that was how things were to be. Others told me that healing was my divine right, that my family and I were suffering unnecessarily, that we were probably under a curse because of something my father or grandfather did.

Well, if I was missing something I wanted to know about it. I thought I knew what the Bible taught about these things, but pain can make you do strange things.

I remember once trying to uproot a bush in our backyard. Our flower garden was expanding, and we needed more room. It was a small, unattractive bush, and it was blocking the progress of the marigolds. The ground was soft; it would be easy to pull up. I wrapped my hands around the base of the bush and gave a mighty heave.

Later, when I was able to straighten up and the pain in my back had subsided, I counted to ten, sucked in air, braced myself, bent over, and gave the mightiest heave within me—followed by a similar effort and then another. Finally my recalcitrant adversary surrendered. As it yielded, a dozen spidery lines of dirt burst from the base of the bush, racing across the lawn in every direction, like moles going to the gold. I wasn't pulling up a little bush—I was pulling up half the backyard.

In like manner, when I pulled on the bush of *healing*, I felt I was pulling at much more than that—something beyond the obvious, visible question of physical healing. Finding the answer about physical healing would not be enough. The real question lay beyond physical healing, and I could not expect to find the right answer unless I asked the right question. Physical healing, I saw, was just the outer layer, a secondary issue. We fancy that we grapple with the ultimate mystery when we take on the question of physical healing—but we do not, for physical healing is not the ultimate issue and certainly not the ultimate achievement. Job, the Old Testament icon of suffering, ultimately understood that as well.

So did my friend Manley Beasley. Manley suffered for twenty years with several terminal diseases, yet through that suffering became one of the greatest men of faith I have known. When approached by a woman who wanted to pray for his healing, he said, "Ma'am, I have long since passed that."

For it is not colds and cancer alone that create the "quiet despair" of life. A broken relationship can hurt more than a broken bone. Many a sick soul resides within a perfectly fit body. "Healthy" people jump out of windows every day.

No, the question is not simply, "Will God heal me of sickness?" It is, "Will God heal me of suffering?" And suffering may be anything that threatens my life or my ability to enjoy it in the fullness God intended. It is more than, "Will God strengthen my leg?" The issue really is, "Will he deepen my faith?"

Will God heal me of my loneliness, my doubt, my "interior hurting?" Will he heal me of worrying about my kids, of the terror of a ringing phone after midnight? Will God make well again injured hearts and restore amputated hopes? Is there deliverance from the meaningless agonies of everyday living, from diseases of the spirit as well as diseases of the body? Is there, this side of heaven, a safe haven from the unexpected cruelties of life, like a protective shield wrapped around us?

Believing in God Can Be a Burden

Pull at the bush a little harder, and another root darts through the dirt: Believing in God can be a burden. Faith creates problems for the believer that others do not have. To believe in a sovereign God who can heal the sick, raise the dead, annihilate the Devil, and launder the earth clean of every blight forces us to face the question: "If he can, why doesn't he? Why doesn't God just release his power and heal all the hurts?" I would, if I were God.

But that's not God's way, we say. Why? Why is that not God's way? He's God. He can make it any way he wants. Why must his way often require my pain?

It is indeed intimidating to realize that thousands of years later we are still asking questions asked by Job and others like him, as though we are the first to admit the mystery. Yet we are no nearer the answers. These are questions that perhaps can never be fully answered in this life, but we ask them. Every generation must ask them for themselves. That includes you and me.

All this makes the subject of this book always relevant. I send it out with the prayer that God will use it to heal the hurt inflicted by erroneous teaching on sickness and healing and to turn the enemy of suffering into the servant of holiness. There is more to suffering than meets the eye.

My Plan

In Part 1, "When Illness Strikes," we will look at how illness affects us as Christians, what we can expect when illness strikes, the stigma that often attaches itself to pain and suffering, the pitfalls of illness, and those who, intentionally or inadvertently, confuse the sick with what I believe to be noncontextual interpretations of God's Word.

In Part 2, "Handling Accurately the Word of Truth," I want to show you some important rules by which you can judge for yourself what the Scriptures teach about divine healing. These guidelines, more than anything else, helped me through the maze of teaching on the subject when sickness, suffering, and death barged into my life. I found no easy, simplistic answers, and I will not offer you such answers in your season of suffering. What I did find, however, was the affirmation of the unequivocal love and sovereignty of God and the peace that results from embracing his ultimate purpose. This is material that gave me peace and hope through the bad times. It can do the same for you.

In Part 3, "Finding God's Good in Suffering," we'll address how to pray for healing and that toughest of issues: when God says no. We'll see how to help a loved one face death and how to conquer fear. And (my favorite part of our journey together) we'll meet and talk with a wonderful man who taught me more about victory in suffering than anyone I've ever known.

To begin, let's talk with some people, folks just like you and me, who have been in the crucible.

CHAPTER 2

The Night Side of Life

The Losses and Gains of Suffering

SHE WAS THIRTY-FIVE, A BEAUTIFUL mother of two, with deep auburn hair and slightly freckled Irish skin. Much of her time was spent in the hot sun, working in her flower garden and small vegetable patch. The sunlight took its toll on her fair skin and a strange red spot appeared on the left side of her face, on the cheek near the nose. Not much for going to doctors, she finally had the strange spot checked out.

"A skin cancer," the doctor said. This was 1953 and cancer treatment was much cruder then. "I'm sending you to Oklahoma City," he said. "They will attach a radium patch to the cancer, and you'll have to wear it until we see what happens."

A week before my mom was to leave for Oklahoma City, she asked me to take some pictures of her. I was fifteen and had a cheap little camera. Puzzled by her request, I was startled when she came out of her bedroom dressed fit to kill. Her face was made up, her hair freshly done, and she was wearing a beautiful white blouse and black silk skirt. I took a full roll of pictures of her standing in front of the fireplace, sitting in a chair, relaxing on the couch—picture after picture, her eyes never looking into the camera but always fixed on some distant object.

When we finished, I asked why she wanted the pictures. She said that she was so afraid of what she might look like after the cancer treatment that she wanted a record of the person she had been.

I still have those pictures. They remind me of the first time I ever saw the fear of a person with a "spoiled identity" syndrome of illness.

You see, sickness is the Great Interrupter of life. It enters without knocking, arresting all plans, mocking the idea of certainty, and diminishing hope for the future. Touching every part of life, sickness takes away parts of you, leaving you to wonder, "Who is the real me?"

Arthur Kleinman says, "The fidelity of our bodies is so basic that we never think of it—it is the certain grounds of our daily experience. Chronic illness is a betrayal of that fundamental trust. We feel under siege: untrusting, resentful of uncertainty, lost. Life becomes a working out of sentiments that follow closely from this corporeal betrayal: confusion, shock, anger, jealousy, despair."[1]

Let me share two stories that illustrate some of the losses and gains we experience during the trauma of serious illness. They may help us to put sickness and its relation to our faith in God in the right perspective.

Julie's Story

Julie is my wife's sister. She is married and the mother of three, a highly successful businesswoman, and one of the finest

Christians I have ever known. In 1986 she was diagnosed with adult celiac sprue, a chronic disorder characterized by malabsorption of food and nutrients. Gluten kills the cells of the small-intestine lining, so healing can come only when the offending gluten is totally removed from the diet. And gluten is in almost everything that tastes good.

On average, it takes a patient nearly fourteen years to get a correct diagnosis. Julie was blessed by a diagnosis within four to six months, but lost thirty-five pounds while the doctors were trying to diagnose the disease. If the disease plays itself out, it results in osteomalacia (softening of the bone tissue) and other problems that result from the lack of any nutrients, which, of course, are necessary to live.

"When faced with sprue," Julie says, "I was confronted with the unknown so long and going downhill while being diagnosed. I always thought there was the possibility of cancer, but during the daily doctor visits and tests and loss of weight, there was an unreality to it all. I felt like I was on a conveyor belt and couldn't get off. I was going down an assembly line I didn't like.

"There was a special aloneness. At the same time as one is faced with thoughts of death, one also faces the horrible, impersonal environment of doctors' offices and hospitals—a lot of sitting and waiting and feeling like only a number—a lot of indignities. Your tests are treated as common and mundane, whereas to you, the results are life and death. You want to scream, 'Doesn't anyone realize how important this is? This is my life!' Instead, you remain quiet and alone with your thoughts; it always turns out to be just you and God. Your world stops, but everyone else's keeps going. In fact, even your own world keeps going; just YOU stop.

"After finally getting a diagnosis of sprue, however, I was so happy to have a disease I could live with instead of die with that

I have never considered it to be much of a burden. It's simply an inconvenience. It's a disease I can be grateful for!"

In 1991, Julie saw a doctor about a mole that had changed shape. After the dermatologist examined her, he left the room. While she waited, she overhead him say, "Let's do the melanoma case first," and then the door burst open. Julie said, "So, you think it's melanoma?"

"Because," Julie says, "I had previously worked for a plastic surgeon who saw melanoma cases for the second follow-up surgery, and because most of those cases were now marked 'deceased,' I stopped the dermatologist from doing the biopsy he was going to do. I didn't want him cutting into the mole. Instead, I insisted he excise it with very wide margins. He was agreeable to do so, and the lab test proved to be malignant melanoma. Thus, when I went to the second surgeon for follow-up, he said the second surgery didn't have to be done. He commented, 'I've never seen a dermatologist do a rotation flap before.' I told him I had insisted on the extremely wide margin. Thus my familiarity with the surgery done by my former employer gave me wisdom in what to ask for."

With the melanoma there was again fear and aloneness.

"I don't think I can say 'aloneness' enough times. There was a desire for every conversation to be deep and meaningful and to talk about death, but of course, it was never mentioned. All talk remained on a surface level, so my thoughts of death and aloneness went unmentioned. In fact, one hour after it was pronounced 'melanoma' I was back at work, wondering if it had spread. I went through the motions of my job. I guess there is a lot of 'going through the motions' at times like this.

"I realized how insignificant I was. I realized my finiteness. I realized my total lack of control. I realized that I was truly in God's hands and the doctor's hands. The fear was the fear of the unknown. The times when I was confronted with the fact that I might become a memory, I was least capable of producing good memories to leave behind.

"In my illnesses, I have never thought, 'Why me?' I have always thought that I have had it too easy in life and haven't had the difficult tests many have had, so my reaction is really, 'Why not me?' Others have had much worse to deal with, so I don't tend to self-pity. When I have been delivered, I have been so overwhelmed with humbleness at being delivered that it is then I wonder, 'Why me? Why am I alive?'"

While there seem to be more gains than losses in Julie's case, that's questionable in the following story.

Greg and Michelle's Story

Greg and Michelle were married on July 28, 1995. Thirty-one-year-old Greg was a Certified Registered Nurse Anesthetist at a local hospital, and his twenty-five-year-old bride was an administrative assistant to one of the pastors of their church. Greg and Michelle spent many hours over hazelnut coffee talking about their dreams for the future. Michelle's greatest desire was to be a wife and mother. Greg's was to build a house.

In early October of that year Greg began to have what he thought was a sinus headache, but he had never had one quite like this. The headache seemed to be located higher, just above the forehead. The pain was persistent over several days and increased in intensity. Greg's ability to complete his thoughts became impaired, and his appetite diminished because of the throbbing pain that became centered in the left side of his head, just a couple of inches above his temple. He awoke on the morning of October 16 with the same symptoms, the stabbing throb undiminished, and he was afraid.

After much persuasion from Michelle, Greg went to the emergency room. CAT and MR scans revealed what Greg's medically educated mind feared: a brain tumor. Just eleven weeks after his marriage, a four-centimeter mass had presented itself in the frontal-parietal area of the left hemisphere of his brain. The neurosurgeon was concerned the tumor could be malignant.

"My medical fears had been confirmed," says Greg, "but it wasn't long before the Lord filled my heart and soul with his peace. God immediately reminded me of my prayer to be a light to my coworkers with whom I was about to spend nine days, for I was admitted to the hospital where I worked.

"Surgery proceeded on October 16 and the Lord reassured me that the surgeon's every move would be under his sovereign control. My only concern was to be a light in the darkness."

"While Greg was thinking of being a light in the darkness," Michelle says, "I was thinking of all the possibilities and hoping for a benign tumor. I, too, experienced peace—peace I knew only the Lord could give. This was one of the many times I would feel God's strength and comfort."

They took Greg into surgery and the wait in ICU began. Five hours later the surgeon pushed open the door and greeted Michelle with unwanted words: "The tumor was successfully removed, but your husband has a terminal cancer—a glioma—grade 4. Unless a Higher Being intervenes, your husband will die."

Greg's brother asked, "How long?"

"Twelve months."

"I will never forget the numbness," Michelle says. "I felt as if someone had just sucked my insides out. Was this real? Was I in a bad dream that I would wake up from, and this would all be over? I left the consultation room feeling almost out-of-body, and I shared the news with family and friends who were waiting anxiously. Waves of emotion soon followed—anger, despair, confusion, hopelessness, fear, fear, fear.

"Greg had made me promise to tell him the truth and as I approached his bed, God again strengthened me. I gently kissed his face and told him what we were facing together. His only response was, 'God knows,' and he squeezed my hand. That was the beginning of our journey with the Lord down cancer's pathway.

"That night was the darkest night of my life. Would I be a widow at twenty-five? I was a newlywed; how could this be happening? My dreams of a home, children, family vacations, our first anniversary, came crashing down around me. The ride of life was spinning out of control and I couldn't stop it or get off. I awoke Tuesday morning in total despair. This was more than I could bear, and it wasn't a dream. It was reality. But God gently wrapped me up that morning, recalling two phrases to my mind: 'Do not be anxious' and 'Be strong and courageous.'

"The week was emotionally, physically, mentally, and spiritually exhausting. People always mean well with their visits and phone calls, but often say stupid and hurtful things. While Greg was resting on medication, I wrestled with what the days ahead would hold. I made lists of questions for the doctors, a list of business things that needed to be done (being newly married, I needed to be made beneficiary of Greg's life insurance policy, and my name needed to be added to our land deed). I bathed Greg, spent hours reading to him from the Word for his comfort and mine, and cried every private moment I had.

"We were looking forward to being home. We couldn't wait to be in the 'normal' world, away from the hospital. But once home, it wasn't normal at all—everything had changed. The two newlyweds who had left the apartment full of hopes, dreams, and unlimited time were no longer the same people. We were a couple struggling to make sense of what was happening. A couple who was no longer dreaming of a house but begging for a future, begging for Greg's life, begging for a miracle.

"Two weeks later we began radiation and chemotherapy. Although Greg did well through therapy, it would bring even more change. Greg's hair fell out in handfuls (it was more traumatic than we expected, but he was cute even when he was bald), his appetite went haywire (we were making night runs to Krystals), and he was easily fatigued. As newlyweds, sex was still new to us as a couple, but now it was physically and emotionally difficult. We ended up just holding each other in tears. We would never be newlyweds again, and what we had become, we weren't sure.

"As the weeks passed, God was faithful to minister through his Word, through cards from believers, encouraging words from friends, hugs from family members, verses on calendars, and even in the sunrise itself—always assuring us of his love for us and his presence in the midst of our dark circumstance.

"We have changed so much. As a young couple we have experienced a depth and intimacy in our relationship that some don't have after fifty years. Not one night passes in which we are not thankful for another day together, no longer taking for granted that we will grow old together. Every moment God gives us on this earth is a blessing. Time has become such a precious commodity; we handle it with care. God has taken our temporal dreams and changed them into eternal ones. We have come to know the Lord Jesus in ways we never would have without the cancer.

"We do not understand why God has allowed Greg to have a deadly brain tumor so early in life, so early in our marriage, and the truth is, we may never know. But through it we have come to know that 'his ways are not our ways,' but we can trust that 'he is good and he doeth good.' Do Greg and I struggle with the possibility of his death? Yes. Do we wish we were just normal? Yes, many times, especially when we pass folks and we hear them whisper, 'He's the guy with cancer.' We are looked at so differently now. Would we volunteer to go through this? No. But would we trade what we've learned along the way? No. Nor would we trade the joy and laughter we shared.

"We still have no ending for our journey. For now, we press on, still hoping, still praying, 'Lord, will you heal us?'"

Losses in Suffering

In every battle there are losses. Even for the victor. Illness is no exception; in fact, the pain, suffering, and uncertainty of serious illness usually amplify the sense of loss experienced by both the patient and the loved ones. Among the most common feelings of loss are:

Loss of Control

This may be the first and most powerful loss the patient feels. Suddenly the body, rather than obeying you, has its own agenda and will behave any way it pleases. You can no longer control the functioning of your own body. It's like driving on an icy highway. Suddenly your car hits an ice slick, and you are out of control. Hit the brakes, twist the steering wheel—nothing helps. All you can do is hang on and wait for the crash. It is a sickening, helpless feeling. The steering wheel and brakes give you the illusion that you are in control of the automobile, and for the most part, you are. But something can happen that wrenches the control from you, and all you can do is hang on for dear life.

We subscribe to the popular notion that life can be managed and we spend hours, even years, mapping out our lives. But life is not an exact science. It cannot be managed, it can only be lived.

But society demands that control be regained. We must work to avoid embarrassing ourselves by being out of control in situations where control is expected. And we must also avoid embarrassing others, who should be protected from the specter of lost body control. If we cannot regain control, then we must conceal it as effectively as possible.

Loss of Identity

Les Tolstoy, in his story *The Death of Ivan Ilyich*, illustrates this loss of identity: "Ivan Ilyich locked the door and started examining himself in a mirror—first full face, then in profile. He took down a portrait of himself with his wife and compared it with what he saw in the mirror. There was a tremendous difference. Then he pulled his sleeves up, bared his arms to the elbows, examined his forearms, and his thoughts grew blacker than night."

Arthur Frank, speaking of his own battle with cancer, says, "I did not dread what I would become, but I needed to mourn the end of what I had been. It was like saying good-bye to a place I had lived in and loved."[2] This is what my mother feared. This is what Ivan Ilyich faced. This is what Julie and Greg and Michelle experienced. People look at you differently. They treat you differently. Friends and family tiptoe in their conversations, afraid they will say the wrong thing. They feel uncomfortable in your presence. You are no longer the person you were; you are the person who has cancer, who is disfigured, who endures chronic pain, who is dying. You are spoiled goods.

In talking to a manic-depressive patient who refused to take her medication, I asked her why.

"How will I know who is the real me?" she answered. "Is the real me the person I am when off the medicine, or is it the real me when I'm on it?"

The Defining Power of Diagnosis

A few words from a doctor can result in a loss of identity, changing a person's view of himself. Here is where we must walk a tightrope. We must not deny the reality of our illness, but neither can we allow that diagnosis to define who we are: "That's the salesman with cancer." "She's a wonderful mother, but she has MS."

To Job's wife and friends, he became defined by his illness. Even those closest to him could not see beyond the scars and sores. He was no longer a person—he was an object of observation and diagnosis, both physical and spiritual.

The Scriptures lead us to believe that the apostle Paul had several physical problems, but he rarely referred to them. When he wrote to the churches, he identified himself as the apostle of Jesus Christ, not as the apostle of Christ with poor eyesight.

Loss of Certainty (If There Is Such a Thing)

When you have a chronic illness, everything you do becomes contingent upon your condition. Vacations are contingent upon your body. You will go to work if your sickness allows it. Even getting up in the morning is stipulated by your sickness. All your plans must have a built-in proviso, for you are no longer certain what your body will do. I remember retired persons who told me of all the plans they had made for retirement—one bought an RV and planned to travel across the United States—only to have the long-laid plans mollified by a crippling disease. What was once predictable is now provisional.

Loss of Place in Society

Thomas Bernhard, in his novel *Wittgenstein's Nephew*, describes the feelings of the sick person leaving the hospital to return to normal living, only to find himself suddenly disenfranchised by his illness. "The returning patient always has a sense of suddenly intruding into a sphere where he no longer has any business."[3] Losses go beyond the body. Sickness often puts a strain on relationships. It is difficult to take some relationships up again, especially with those who could not acknowledge your illness. It is surprising how those with serious illnesses form new friendships with those who have been likewise afflicted. Arthur Frank says, "During cancer I felt I had no right to be among others. As much as I disliked being in the hospital, at least there I felt I belonged."[4]

These losses are great and very real, exacting a severe toll on the sufferer. But as we surrender ourselves and our situation to God, entrusting him with our lives, we can overcome these losses through the sufficiency of Christ.

Gains in Suffering

The Chinese believe that before you can conquer a beast, you must first make it beautiful. It may sound contradictory, but for all the losses we incur in illness, we also have an opportunity to gain. You may mourn your losses, but you do not allow these losses to obscure your sense of what you can become. You may curse your fate, but you must also count your possibilities.

Clarified Values

Remember Julie's desire for every conversation to be meaningful? And her overwhelming sense of her finiteness? Remember how Greg and Michelle grew to cherish every moment together, thanking God every day for one more day of life? One of the things that has so impressed me as I talk to people with life-threatening illnesses is the fact that they often say the sickness is worth what they learned from it, about themselves and about God. I'm sure not every ill person feels that way, but those who do not are missing one of the great blessings of life.

Few things focus the mind like being diagnosed with a deadly disease. Being a minister for forty years has given me the awesome privilege of standing by the bedside of many a saint as they have gone to meet God. I've talked to many businessmen as they lay dying. And do you know what? None have ever said to me, "Oh, Pastor, I wish I had spent more time at the office." You know what they say? "Oh, Pastor, I wish I had spent more time with my family."

I remember that after my mother had been diagnosed with cancer, she talked to me about noticing the leaf on a tree, how green a blade of grass was, the shape of clouds, the song of a bird, and the design on a rose. Her senses were tremendously heightened. Often only after being confronted with a life-threatening illness do we realize the price tags *have truly* been switched and that most of our labor has been in the junk business.

Renewal

Recovery may not be possible in every case but renewal is. The opportunity for reexamination and revaluation of the life you have been living and the values you have lived for offers you the chance to choose the new life you will lead, rather than simply living out the one you have accumulated over the years. In short, you answer the question," Is what I have been living for worth dying for?" Even for terminal patients, whatever time may be left to them can be spent living out a renewed life. Renewal comes from a fresh encounter with God, a new appreciation of his Word and his grace, a higher regard for friends and fellowship.

Freedom

This may appear strange, but let Arthur Frank again speak to us. "Within the year [of my illness] I would learn that the ill or impaired may, in the sense of fulfilling life, be far more free than healthy people . . . The ill accept their vulnerability . . . and this acceptance is their freedom."[5]

As much as I appreciate good health, if I make it a requirement for a happy life, then I am enslaved to the fickleness of life and the unpredictability of my body. If in the growth process I have been brought up to believe that "prosperity" is the norm and my right, I will be flattened when I slam into the wall of reality. It takes time to recover from this surprising assault on my beliefs. Then gradually I begin to recover, learning that real life doesn't require "prosperity."

I must ask myself the question: Does my happiness, my joy, my feeling of worth depend on being healthy? We are free when we no longer require health, however much we prefer it, to be happy and at peace.

A New and Deeper Trust in God

Consider a remarkable statement by the apostle Paul in 2 Corinthians. In the opening chapter, verses 3 through 11, he speaks of great adversity in his life: "For we do not want you to be unaware, brethren, of our affliction which came to us in Asia, *that we were burdened excessively, beyond our strength, so that we despaired even of life"* (v. 8). He does not tell us what this affliction was, but he was so utterly, unbearably crushed that he despaired of life itself. "Indeed," he says in verse 9, "we had the sentence of death within ourselves." A better translation might be, "We had the answer of death." As Paul cried out in the midst of this affliction, the only answer he received was like, "You're going to die." And then he says he has this answer, *"So that we would not trust in ourselves, but in God who raises the dead"* (v. 9).

"So that we should stop trusting in ourselves, but in God." Don't you find that an amazing admission? Paul was trusting in himself, and God was trying to teach the apostle to trust in him. Now that wouldn't be so remarkable if these were the words of a novice, but Paul is no novice, is he? This is the great apostle who has already written part of the Holy Scriptures, who has been caught up into the third heaven and shown wonders that cannot be told. He has seen people healed and raised from the dead. And yet, do you mean that even at this stage in his career, he was still having to learn to trust in God? I would have thought that by this time he would have perfected that virtue.

I think this was a lifelong problem with Paul—this trusting in himself. He was so clever, so gifted, so strong that it was natural for him to lean on his own abilities. And if the great apostle had trouble at times relying on himself rather than God how much more do we? Yet notice it was through great affliction that God was teaching him to trust in the Lord.

This has been the recurring theme of the testimonies in this chapter and will be so throughout this book. Let's face it, most of us will not trust God until we have to. As long as we have one more dollar in the bank, one more how-to-book to read, one more seminar to attend, one more trick up our sleeve, we will not trust God.

But it is not the praises of prosperity that impress me, but the praises that come from adversity. That is why I'm delighted that you have chosen to join me as we explore the deeper, "God-ultimate purpose" of sickness, suffering, and even death. For it is as we discover and embrace the work God is intending to do in us, that we can also accept his method of reaching us—and experience deeper faith, stronger courage, and even more genuine joy in the midst of suffering.

CHAPTER 3

Where Does Sickness Come From?

Is God in Sovereign Control of His Universe?

HAVE YOU EVER FELT LIKE saying "It isn't fair!" as you struggled with an illness or a longtime affliction? I'm sure we all have.

As you look about, you see a man who is godless, wicked—and healthy. You also see the saintliest of saints enduring one blast of suffering after another. It is not surprising that philosophers, theologians, and ordinary folks like us have struggled for centuries to solve this puzzle.

The quest has yielded some answers. Some, of course, are oversimplified, and we should always be wary of simple answers to complex problems. For example, one writer offers this explanation: "When a person becomes sick, he has in some way violated the laws of health. For that person to get well, he must cooperate with that same law."[1] When I read that to my doctor, he was really impressed. "It sounds so good," he said, "so simple, so true. Too bad it isn't."

This answer is naïve and unsatisfying, for it fails to take into account the person who, through no fault of his own, inherits a genetic deficiency from his parents that results in a severe illness. Obeying every health law in the book would not have prevented that, nor would it produce a cure.

Nor can anyone ever be absolutely sure what the proper health laws are. Even the medical profession constantly changes its opinions of those. My wife, for instance, was told by her doctor to eat liver because she was suffering from an iron deficiency. Yet we are now told that liver is a fatty food with a high level of cholesterol that can cause heart problems.

Since a sick person may not know which health laws he violated, he doesn't know which ones to cooperate with to bring about a cure.

Kaye loves to walk several miles every day (I drive the pace car), but a long rainy season kept her indoors. To compensate, she bought a mini-trampoline. One day while she was shopping, I sat in the car reading a very interesting news article. The headline said, "Tests on Animals Show Link with Exercise, Cancer." Researchers at the Membrane Bioenergetics Group at the University of California found in tests on animals (rats and guinea pigs) that physical exercise generates massive bursts of agents that have been linked to cancer and aging. Dr. Lester Packer said, "The more we research, the more evident it becomes that risk is present in everything and that in the end it will come to a question of trade-offs."[2]

We have all known or heard of people who seemed to be perfect physical specimens: They ate the right food, got plenty of sleep, exercised religiously, refrained from smoking and drinking, lived in a nuclear-free zone—and dropped dead on the jogging trail. I'll never forget a picture I saw in a 1960s newspaper on the same day the Surgeon General's report came out informing the public of the life-shortening potential of smoking. On the same page as that report was a picture of the famous author Somerset Maugham, celebrating his ninetieth birthday, with a cigarette dangling from his mouth.

By far the favorite explanation for sickness, and the one most espoused by those who believe that illness cannot be part of God's will, is Satan. Sickness, they say, is always caused by sin and delivered to man by Satan. And since sickness is from the Devil, it must be contrary to the will of God. Conclusion? It is always God's will to heal.

God Is Absolutely Sovereign

While Satan may be able to cause sickness, it is a moot point because the Bible teaches that God is the absolute Sovereign over everything, even the Devil. Satan can operate only within the limits God sets for him. Witness the case of Job. The Devil himself could not touch him without divine permission, and then only within the limits prescribed by God (see Job 1:12; 2:6). We are not at odds with scriptural teaching to say that God often uses evil and the Evil One to accomplish his redemptive purposes. "For the wrath of man shall praise You" (Ps. 76:10).

The prophet Isaiah portrays godless Assyria as the instrument of God's wrath when he records, "Woe to Assyria, the rod of My anger and the staff in whose hands is My indignation, I send it against a godless nation and commission it against the people of My fury. . . . Yet it does not so intend; nor does it plan so in its heart" (Isa. 10:5–7). The nation of Assyria is pictured as the unconscious servant of the Lord, an unwitting pawn in the strategy of redemption.

The same was true of Cyrus: "Thus says the LORD to Cyrus His anointed, whom I have taken by the right hand, to subdue nations before him and to loose the loins of kings . . . I have also called you by your name; I have given you a title of honor though you have not known Me . . . I will gird you, though you have not known Me" (Isa. 45:1, 4–5).

When Habakkuk complained that God was doing nothing while the nation decayed internally and was threatened by destruction externally from the Chaldeans, God responded by saying, "Look among the nations! Observe! Be astonished! Wonder! Because I am doing something in your days—you would not believe if you were told. For behold, I am raising up the Chaldeans" (Hab. 1:5–6).

In his book *Faith Healing and the Christian Faith*, Wade H. Boggs tells us that: "Evil men, who live in rebellion against God, are nevertheless compelled to serve Him as involuntary instruments, for God can weave even the wicked into His design. . . . In like manner, the Devil is under the power of God, so that while he is fighting against God, he is compelled to be the involuntary instrument of His purpose."[3]

The person of Satan and the principle of evil are often seen as God-recognized ingredients in his government of this world and are presented at times as his servants rather than his enemies. King Saul felt the business end of this truth when "the Spirit of the LORD departed from Saul, and *an evil spirit from the LORD terrorized him*" (1 Sam. 16:14).

Let me put forward some questions. Does God have to put up with the Devil? Is God in sovereign control of his universe? If he wanted to, couldn't he get rid of Satan? I can only answer yes to these questions, which leads me to believe that if Satan did not serve a useful purpose in the scheme of God's redemptive program, he would nuke him.

Satan Isn't Responsible for All Physical Malfunction

That's why I think it is wrong to attribute every kind of physical malfunction to the Devil, demons, or curses. Recently I heard an evangelist say that arthritis was a curse placed upon people because of something their grandparents had done. Currently popular among some is the idea that everything from arthritis to migraine headaches is a result of a curse received from parents or grandparents, and that before healing or deliverance can be obtained, these satanic curses must be broken. In Old Testament times there was a popular proverb, oft-quoted because it let people off the hook. It went something like this: "The fathers have eaten sour grapes, and the children's teeth are set on edge" (Jer. 31:29). In other words, the children were not responsible for their actions; they were simply being punished for what their parents had done. But under the new covenant, which Christ would establish by his shed blood, those words would not be spoken again: "Everyone will die for his own iniquity; each man who eats the sour grapes, his teeth will be set on edge" (Jer. 31:30).

I agree with M. Scott Peck who, when writing of "The Sins of the Fathers" syndrome, says, "It is the parents themselves who visit their sins upon their children."[4]

And then there was the family of our acquaintance whose children had several bouts with sickness. The cause of this sickness, they were told, was the mother's collection of owl statuettes. It was these graven images that gave the demons a point of contact, a beachhead into the home. The owls were destroyed. The children remained sick.

It is frightening to see how far some go in this area. Instead of New Testament Christianity, it is more of a voodoo religion built on superstition and may itself be the real demonic channel into a life or home.

J. I. Packer writes, "If life is seen as a battle with demons in such a way that Satan and his hosts get blamed for bad health, bad thoughts and bad behavior, without reference to physical, psychological and rational factors in the situation, a very unhealthy demonic counterpart of the supernaturalism is being developed. There is no doubt that this sometimes happens and that it is a major obstacle to moral and spiritual maturity when it does."[5]

I'll never forget the pastor in Kansas years ago who asked me if I had a recorded sermon series on the Devil, demons, and the occult. I replied that I did.

"How much is the whole set?" he asked.

"Thirteen dollars," I said.

He paused and considered. "Could I write you a check for twelve dollars and owe you a dollar?" he asked

"Well, I guess so," I said. "But why?"

He hesitated, then said, "I don't like to write checks for *thirteen* dollars."

This was a preacher. He really needed the sermon series. Probably I should have given them to him. Instead, I said, "Tell you what—write me a check for fourteen dollars and I'll owe *you* one."

And he did. Anything to avoid dealing with the number thirteen.

The Thorny Problem of the Thorn

Much has been made of Paul's thorn in the flesh as a "messenger of Satan" (2 Cor. 12:7). While we can only speculate as to the nature of the physical malady described as a thorn, there are some things we can say about it with certainty.

1. It was a gift. "There was *given* me a thorn in the flesh." Through the process of prayer and communion, the apostle stopped pleading for its removal and accepted it as a gift of God's grace.

2. Twice the apostle mentions the reason for the gift of the thorn: "to keep me from exalting myself." I find it difficult to believe that the Devil would do anything for the purpose of keeping one of God's servants humble.

3. Paul's response to the thorn was to glory, not grumble. "Most gladly, therefore, I will rather boast about my weakness" (v. 9). The thorn, instead of a hindrance (as Paul first perceived it), proved to be an advantage. Would the great apostle glory in the work of the Devil? I doubt it.

From a new viewpoint a familiar landscape can sometimes look very different. And often the things in our lives we consider a hindrance may be the very thing that God is using to make us more useful to him. Isn't that what we all should desire?

Granted, Paul does call the thorn a "messenger of Satan," but that only reinforces what we have been saying about God's sovereignty. The thorn was a messenger of Satan in that Satan delivered it, but God sent it. (Don't you think it would make the Devil steam if he knew he was God's delivery boy?) It originated with God, was a gift of God sent to accomplish the purpose of God. As A. J. Gordon, a pastor during the late 1800's, once said,

"The Lord sometimes allows His saints to be sharpened on the Devil's grindstone."

Wade Boggs tells us: "In the light of such teaching from scripture, we may advise the sick Christian to waste no time worrying over the possibility that he is the helpless victim of malevolent spirits; rather let him turn his thoughts to the power and goodness of God, and ask what good thing God is trying to teach him through this experience."[6]

But Where Does Sickness Come From?

I prefer to write *mystery* over the whole issue, for I have the feeling that the wisest of human minds is incompetent to solve the puzzle. But, to prove that fools rush in where angels fear to tread, I will risk being simplistic and offer what I believe are the four basic sources of sickness.

1. *God.* That's right. I believe God himself is often the source of illness. To say that he *permits* it but does not *cause* it, and to the one suffering, it amounts to the same thing.

In Exodus 15:26, God makes a promise to his people. If they will pledge obedience to his commandments, he promises, "I will put none of the diseases on you which I have put on the Egyptians." He had already inflicted certain diseases on the Egyptians, and if the Hebrews didn't shape up, he would do the same to them.

In Deuteronomy 28, we read that if the people do not give careful obedience to God's Word, "then the LORD will bring extraordinary plagues on you and your descendants, even severe and lasting plagues, and miserable and chronic sicknesses" (Deut. 28:59).

It is obvious in these two instances that sickness would be used by God as a means of chastening and judgment. In the case of Job it was for different reasons, and it is interesting that Job never gives credit to Satan for anything that befell him. He considers it all from the hand of God. Paul's thorn in the flesh, as we have seen, was a gift from God. So for whatever reason he chose, whether we understand it or not, there are occasions when God himself is the source of sickness and suffering.

2. *Satan.* In Luke 13, Jesus healed a woman "who for eighteen years had had a sickness caused by a spirit" (v. 11). Later, when he was criticized for healing on the Sabbath, Jesus said, "And this woman, a daughter of Abraham as she is, whom Satan has bound for eighteen long years, should she not have been released from this bond on the Sabbath day?" (v. 16).

Satan can inflict a person with sickness, but, as we have seen, we must not assume that every and all sickness is the work of a demon. Matthew is careful to distinguish between demon-possession and sickness in Matthew 4:24: "The news about Him spread throughout all Syria; and they brought to Him all who were ill, those suffering with various diseases and pains, demoniacs, epileptics, paralytics; and He healed them."

3. *Our personal lifestyle.* Our bodies are so constituted that if we flagrantly disregard the laws of health, the body will react in illness. In the introduction to his book *The American Way of Life Need Not Be Hazardous to Your Health*, Dr. John Farquhar states, "Often we assume that our lifestyle is healthy, that everything is 'normal,' when in fact we're following a path inimical to our health . . . Ill health is not an isolated event; it is the result of an

accumulation of abuses, each seemingly inconsequential. Eventually they take their toll. . . . In the way we live our daily lives, we either enhance our health or diminish it."[7]

If you smoke four packs of cigarettes a day for twenty years and come down with lung cancer, you can't blame it on God, Satan, or the tobacco industry. You did it to yourself.

If a person gorges himself into obesity and high blood pressure and drops dead of a heart attack, he can't say that it was God or Satan. It was his lifestyle.

An alcoholic can't blame his bad liver on anyone but himself. As Paul Tournier puts it, "Most illnesses do not, as generally thought, come like a bolt out of the blue. The groundwork is prepared for years, through faulty diet, intemperance, overwork, and moral conflicts, slowly eroding the subject's vitality. And when at last the illness suddenly shows itself, it would be a most superficial medicine which treated it without going back to its remote causes."[8]

4. *Being a human.* There is a natural process of decay going on right now in your body. Let's face it, sickness goes with the territory. Being a Christian does not make us immune to the frailties of the flesh; we are still part of the human situation, and the "outer man is decaying" (2 Cor. 4:16). We should not expect there to be a big, mysterious, supernatural explanation for everything that happens in our life. I like the way Philip Yancey puts it: "The natural laws which rule this planet are, on the whole, good laws which fit the design God has for men and women. And becoming a Christian does not equip us with a germ-free, hermetically sealed space suit to protect us from the dangers of earth."[9]

Some years ago a young man in our church, a lay preacher, was visiting a nursing home when he came to the bed of an invalid woman in her late eighties. Having been confined to her bed for several years, she was understandably in a dark mood. When he greeted her, she asked, "Are you a preacher?"

"Well, yes, I am," he replied.

"Then maybe you can tell me."

"Tell you what?"

"What I'm doing here like this," she said. "All my life I've been a Christian and done my best to serve the Lord. I was a member of the church, taught Sunday school, sang in the choir. Raised my kids to be Christians. Now look at me, will you? Why? Why am I here like this? Can you tell me?"

"Yes, I can," the young man answered.

"You can!" It was a question she obviously asked every preacher who came by. But now here was one who knew the real secret behind her plight. "Tell me, Brother. Why am I here like this?"

Smiling, he took her hand and said gently, "Old age."

We are part of a fallen race; we live in a sinful society. And it sometimes happens that the innocent suffer with the guilty. All too often moral people are the victims of an immoral world. As Christians we are no more exempt from the calamities and catastrophes of life than non-Christians. If I'm driving down the street and run a stop sign and a truck broadsides me, it is ridiculous to claim that it was Satan or demons who caused the accident, or that it was the result of some secret sin in my life. To discover the cause, I need look no further than my own carelessness.

God has not promised that disaster will not find its way to believers. But he has promised us grace to bear it and to use it for our good and his glory. Or as Augustine wisely observed, "God judged it better to bring good out of evil than to suffer evil not to exist."

CHAPTER 4

By the Rivers of Babylon

The Modern-Day Stigmas
of Sickness

IT IS NOT COOL TO be sick.

It was a beautiful spring day in 1986 in Tulsa, Oklahoma, and I was going mad. My ten-year struggle with the black hole of depression, with its rage, anxiety, panic attacks, failure of memory and concentration, loss of interest in nearly everything, preoccupation with death and suicide, deprivation of energy and sleep, had pushed me to the dark edge of insanity.

Kaye had tried to get me to see a psychiatrist, but I knew that I could beat this thing—after all, I was a Christian and a minister at that.

My greatest fear was that I might be found out. Finally, however, I recognized that if I were to survive, I had no choice. So I called Kaye from Tulsa and told her to set up an appointment with the Christian psychiatrist she had told me about. And sure enough, when I walked into the doctor's office, I found to my dismay that the receptionist was a former member of my church.

There was no place to hide, to avoid being labeled, stigmatized. The greatest fear of the ill person, that of being labeled, was mine.

The New Social Evil

Our preoccupation with the body beautiful and mass media's emphasis on youth and beauty have spawned a new social evil: sickness. Sickness is out of style. It is a stigma.

Stigma is a word derived from the practice of branding slaves, especially those who had run away or otherwise disobeyed their master. It came to mean a sign on the surface of the body signifying danger, guilt, or uncleanness. Arthur Frank says, "Stigmas began as judicial punishments in the form of notched ears, brandings, and other visible mutilations of the body. These marks allowed those who came into contact with the stigmatized person to see who they were dealing with. The stigmatized were expected to go to the margins of society and hide their spoiled bodies. The causes of stigmatization have changed, but the hiding has not."[1]

Have you ever felt stigmatized yourself? Or, even subconsciously, allowed yourself to think this way about an acquaintance who was experiencing severe physical or emotional pain? There is no denying that it happens to the best of us and that it emanates from even the most well-intentioned people. And the stigma we place on the sick is a major factor in why we (mistakenly) believe that God also turns his back on illness—that he would have no good purpose for our suffering.

The Social Stigma

Illness of any kind, of the body, mind, or spirit, even of the pocketbook, has become a social and spiritual stigma, producing what Dr. David Rabin called "The Pariah Syndrome."

Dr. Rabin gives a moving testimony when he writes of the social consequences of his own disease, amyotrophic lateral sclerosis (ALS)—better known as Lou Gehrig's Disease: "However, what we did not fully appreciate was that ALS, or for that matter any chronic incurable illness, also induces a social disease. Patients and their families become pariahs, cast off by many in society who are unable to face them. Thus, they contend not only with their illness but also the response it evokes."

Describing his sudden isolation from friends and colleagues, Dr. Rabin said, "The message was quite clear—my illness had resulted in the irrevocable cancellation of what Susan Sontag has called 'the passport of the healthy.' Lacking this, my family and I were excluded by a rather large group of people. We had been reclassified as pariahs, social outcasts."[2]

In his book *Wrestling with the Angel*, columnist Max Lerner tells of his battle with prostate cancer:

> Understandable there is the smell of taboo around life-threatening maladies, since a society tribally tries to protect its integrity and sees a stricken person as a threat to the well-being of all. Very early, and throughout my illness, I tried to be honest about my cancer with myself and others. I paid a price for my openness. As word spread, my lecture requests and magazine assignments melted away. Max Lerner in his late seventies presented quite an image from Max Lerner with cancer—and God knows what else—on his way out of life's arena. We immure our sick in the hospitals but we also invent ingenious ways of moving them offstage, banishing them from life's center, making their healing more difficult.[3]

Simone Weil, herself a sufferer, observed that people by nature respond to the afflicted as hens who rush upon a wounded hen with slashing beaks. Everybody, she said, "despises the afflicted to some extent, although practically no one is conscious of it."[4]

A Spoiled Identity

In our day the *stigma* has come to refer less to the bodily mark and more to the *disgrace* of the mark. Society's attitude toward sickness transmits to the sick person the feeling of a spoiled identity, a feeling of being inferior, a deviant, almost a freak.[5]

Have you ever been depressed enough to read one of Franz Kafka's stories? You don't *have* to be depressed, but it helps. Anyway, a good one to read for our purposes is "The Metamorphosis," in which the hero, Gregor Samsa, wakes up one morning to discover that he has turned into a giant insect. (See now why I said being depressed helps?) This story is a metaphor of illness, because I guarantee you if you wake up in the morning having turned into a big bug, something is definitely wrong.

When Gregor awakens, he's lying on his back with six stubby legs flailing the air. Getting out of bed, he falls and seriously injures himself. Later, his father throws an apple at him to drive him back into his room; the apple lodges in his back and festers so that he is barely able to move.

Gregor Samsa has become a pariah, stigmatized and outcast. For our discussion, it is the reaction of the family that is most instructive. Stricken with the horror of what has happened to a member of their family, they pass through several stages.

First, there is *shock and disbelief.* How are they supposed to react to this tragedy? What has happened is a total denial of their idea of what a normal family should be. Having no background of dealing with tragedy, no family traditions in this sort of thing, the only thing they can do is deny it. But denial cannot be long sustained when you've got a big bug living in the bedroom.

The second stage is *help and caring*. Since they still cannot bear the sight of him, they appreciate it when he hides himself when they enter the room to feed him. They even rearrange the furniture so he will have more room to move around.

But as hope for a change dims, their caring stage shifts to resentment. His room is neglected, allowed to become filthy, and eventually used as a storage dump, and the food he is given is wholly inadequate. Finally, his sister says they should stop kidding themselves—this insect is not their brother.

The final stage is both *grief and relief* when Gregor dies. Howard Brody says that the family members view Gregor's sickness as something that happened to them, not as something that happened to Gregor, the effects of which they must share.[6] This insight makes it clear why Gregor's family must regard him as a pariah, a stigma, something shameful that must be hidden away. Thus an essential element in suffering is the social degradation, isolation, and ostracism.

"Eventually," writes Arthur Kleinman, "the stigmatized person comes to expect such reactions, to anticipate them before they occur or even when they don't occur. By that stage, he has thoroughly internalized the stigma in a deep sense of shame and a spoiled identity."[7]

The New Lepers

In the early years of the previous century it was tuberculosis that everyone feared and ran from. Then cancer became the major taboo (even though heart disease takes more lives).

Today the cry of "Unclean!" belongs to those who have AIDS. For our generation this has become the ultimate leprosy. Families of AIDS sufferers have not only been ostracized from their communities, their houses have been burned, they have been fired from their jobs and removed from their schools. Many have been forced to relocate to a different state to escape the harassment and stigma.

Jimmy Allen, past president of the world's largest Protestant denomination, Southern Baptists, tells his poignant story in his book *Burden of a Secret.*

His daughter-in-law, Lydia, had to receive several blood transfusions during a difficult childbirth. Several years later they found out one of the transfusions had been tainted with the HIV virus. Lydia and her newborn son, Matt, left the hospital unknowingly carrying the virus. Several years later she gave birth to another son, Bryan, who was also born with the virus. Through a series of circumstances, they later discovered that Lydia, Matthew, and Bryan had AIDS.

Dr. Allen's son, Scott, the husband and father, was on the staff of a Christian church in Colorado. Feeling it was the right thing to do, he informed the pastor, who immediately fired him. The family was told not to return to the church. Fear and ignorance reigned wherever the young Allen family went. Bryan died first, then Lydia, and more recently, Matt. Although they did find Christian friends who embraced them, the story is a powerful testimony to the destructive power of stigma.[8]

Ironically, the gay community is largely to blame for the mass hysteria concerning AIDS. In their understandable efforts to raise public awareness of the disease and funds for research and treatment, they engaged in overkill, painting such a horrible picture of the threat ("Everyone is at risk!") of this new malady that the American people became terrified—to the point of ostracizing

AIDS patients more than ever. Much of that has changed in recent years, and progress has been made in providing help and comfort to victims of AIDS. But it remains the ultimate stigma.

296.33

That's me. If you look up that number in the DSM-IV-R (the Diagnostical and Statistical Manual of Mental Disorders), you'll find these words: *Major Depression, recurrent, severe.* That's the diagnosis of my illness.

In 1993 I spoke to fifteen hundred ministers and their wives on behalf of the health-care organization Rapha. At the beginning of my speech I didn't know if I should mention my depression, the psychiatric care, and ongoing medication. But I had come to the place where my life and family meant more than the judgment of others, so I told them. It was hard, but I told them. I will forever be grateful for the wife of a minister friend who approached me immediately after the meeting and, with tears in her eyes, said, "Don't ever regret saying what you said here today." As a result of that speech and the subsequent disclosure of my problem in my book *When Heaven Is Silent*, hundreds have sought me out to tell their own similar stories. I was astonished to learn of so many who have been forced to suffer in silence because of the fear of stigma.

At any one moment in this nation about thirty million people suffer from some form of mental or emotional disorder. The stigma of these disorders is probably second only to that of AIDS. Depression, manic-depressive illness, and other emotional disorders always beget fear, suspicion, distrust, and alienation in our society. Depression and its kinfolk are usually considered signs of weakness—these "whining people just need to get their act together and shape up."

But the truth about depression and manic-depressive illnesses is that they are just that: illnesses, biological, medical, real, "I'm telling the truth" illnesses; a genetic disease caused by some biochemical imbalance in the brain. While doctors disagree on some aspects of the causes, most agree to the basic facts. The brain has chemical messengers called neurotransmitters, and when these transmitters are healthy and normal, we are too. But the absence of one or more of three chemical transmitters—serotonin, norepinephrine, or dopamine—can trigger major depression. Depression may come on at any age, striking women twice as often as men, and affecting up to 10 percent of the population at some time in their lives.

Depression may affect the victim in many ways—from deep feelings of sadness, guilt, uselessness, worthlessness, and futility to impaired memory and poor concentration. A sense of losing one's mind is not uncommon. Uncontrollable tears, profound apathy, fatigue often occur, along with appetite changes, dehydration, and severe weight loss. Suicide is a constant risk and sleep often unattainable.

The good news about depression is that help is available. You don't have to feel that way. A combination of medication and psychotherapy can make a normal life possible. "The best brain in the world," writes Wilfred Sheed, "cannot think its way out of depression, because all its ideas are poisoned at the source."[9]

Unfortunately, there is such stigma attached to mental disorders that many, if not most, of those afflicted refuse to get help. Again, their depressed state is seen as a sign of weakness and medication as a crutch. In the case of treating manic-depressive illness (which is highly treatable), the number-one problem is getting the patients to take their medicine. Most fail to get help because they fear exposure, believing that exposure will lead to rejection.

An Unbiblical Mind-Body Split

I think one reason we have so much trouble with this issue is that we have a mind-body split. If we think of the self as all one (although with different dimensions—a tri-unity rather than a trinity), then we would tackle the physical at the same time as the spiritual, knowing that it is all interrelated.

But if we go on thinking there is just a spiritual problem, then that is a form of dualism, which for the Christian disavows the Incarnation. Christianity says the body is real. If we see Jesus as meaning anything at all, it's an Incarnation in the flesh. Therefore, a depressed Christian ought to seek the help both of a medical and a spiritual counselor.[10]

One of the world's foremost authorities on manic-depressive illness, also known as bipolar disorder, is Kay Redfield Jamison, professor of psychiatry at Johns Hopkins University School of Medicine. She coauthored the standard medical text on manic-depressive illness.

In 1995 Dr. Jamison wrote *An Unquiet Mind*, in which for the first time she publicly described her own manic depression, which had plagued her since the age of seventeen. Describing the illness, she says, "Manic depression distorts moods and thoughts, incites dreadful behaviors, destroys the basis of rational thought, and too often erodes the desire and will to live. It is an illness that is biological in its origins, yet one feels psychological in the experience of it; an illness that is unique in conferring advantage and pleasure, yet one that brings in its wake almost unendurable suffering and, not infrequently, suicide."[11]

Most interesting to me was what she had to say about her concerns in writing the book:

> I have had many concerns about writing a
> book that so explicitly describes my own attacks
> of mania, depression, and psychosis, as well as
> my problem acknowledging the need for ongoing
> medication. Clinicians have been, for obvious rea-
> sons of licensing and hospital privileges, reluctant
> to make their psychiatric problems known to oth-
> ers. These concerns are often well warranted. I have
> no idea what the long-term effects of discussing
> such issues so openly will be on my personal and
> professional life, but, whatever the consequences,
> they are bound to be better than continuing to be
> silent. I am tired of hiding, tired of misspent and
> knotted energies, tired of the hypocrisy, and tired
> of acting as though I have something to hide. One
> is what one is, and the dishonesty of hiding behind
> a degree, or title, or any manner and collection of
> words, is still exactly that" dishonest. . . . I continue
> to have concerns about my decision to be pub-
> lic about my illness, but one of the advantages of
> having had manic-depressive illness for more than
> thirty years is that very little seems insurmount-
> ably difficult. . . . I find myself somewhat inevitably
> taking a certain solace in Robert Lowell's essential
> question, *"Yet why not say what happened?"*[12]

By the Rivers of Babylon

To me one of the most beautiful and meaningful passages in the Bible is found in Psalm 137: "By the rivers of Babylon, there we sat down, yea, we wept, when we remembered Zion. . . . How shall we sing the LORD's song in a strange land?" (vv 1, 4 KJV). Many who suddenly discover they have a chronic or acute illness are like the Israelites—they find themselves in a strange land as they sit by the "rivers of Babylon and weep," remembering their days of wholeness. How can they sing in that strange land?

Because of the stigma of some illnesses, especially depression, we are afraid to voice what is happening to us, afraid that people will picture us stumbling around in our pajamas, eyes glazed, mouth drooling, muttering to ourselves, and carrying on conversations with Churchill's black dog and Kafka's mice.

But those sitting by the rivers of Babylon must be allowed to weep, and we who hear must embrace them.

The Spiritual Stigma

Overlapping the social stigma, yet separate from it, is the spiritual stigma that is often attached to illness. The isolation of illness is often made even more acute in religious circles, where sickness is looked upon as an evidence of spiritual deficiency. A number of years ago I released a set of audio tapes on divine healing. Shortly after their release I became plagued with some chronic physical problems. Word reached me that some colleagues were saying that my sickness was punishment from God for things I said in the tapes.

I remember a young mother in Little Rock, Arkansas, standing in the foyer of a church with her two little daughters, telling me that friends had informed her that her husband, who had died the year before from cancer, "had not died from cancer, but from her unbelief."

A friend of mine was called to a new place of service, but a heart attack delayed his arrival for several weeks. Some in the church said his heart attack was a sign from God that he was the wrong man for the position.

Sheila Walsh, an internationally known recording artist and author and cohost on *The 700 Club*, says that when she entered the hospital for depression some coworkers said to her such things as:

> "Do you know the damage you are doing to the
>   ministry?"
> "I always knew you would lose it someday"
> "You might never be special again."[13]

In recent years it has been popular in some evangelical-fundamentalist circles to rail against seeking help from psychologists and psychiatrists, labeling them as "of the Devil."

Just a few years ago Kaye and I, sharing a Bible conference in Louisiana, listened to one of the speakers savagely denounce all psychological and psychiatric professionals. "There is no such thing as a Christian psychologist," he shouted. Holding his red Bible above his head and waving it in the air, he said, "All you need is this book!"

It was hard for us to sit there and listen. Our oldest son had committed suicide as a result of manic depression, and God had saved my own life and ministry through the help of psychiatrists and medication.

One can possibly understand the stigma laid upon the sick person by the world. It is a stigma born largely of fear, ignorance, and uneasiness.

But it is, for me at least, almost impossible to understand the stigma that many Christians attach to other Christians struck by illness. The stigma attached to Christians by many fellow believers is born not only out of ignorance, but also out of spiritual pride and arrogance, devoid of understanding and compassion. The stigmatized Christian is wounded in the house of his friends.

I have counseled countless believers who deny their pain and forego any treatment, hiding their suffering lest they be labeled as unspiritual, lacking in faith and harboring some secret sin. As Sheila Walsh said, "No intelligent person would condemn someone for having a brain tumor, so why do so many people discount or distance themselves from a different form of trouble?"[14]

I may sound impassioned about this, but I have listened to too many people who wear on their faces the harsh graffiti of silent suffering. The Christian community's lack of understanding and support doesn't allow these dear people to voice their pain—and if suffering must be hidden in the basement of the heart, it doubles the pain.

Is There Help?

Is there a way to stop stigmatizing people? Yes. It is the way of the apostle James. In the second chapter of his epistle he condemns showing preference to certain people because they appear superior to others. If we do this, he asks, "Have you not made distinctions among yourselves, and become judges with evil motives? . . . If, however, you are fulfilling the royal law according to the Scripture, 'YOU SHALL LOVE YOUR NEIGHBOR AS YOURSELF,' you are doing well. But if you show partiality, you are committing sin and are convicted by the law as transgressors" (James 2:4, 8–9).

For you who are victims of stigmatization, I would remind you that you are accepted by the only One who really counts:

"To the praise of the glory of his grace, wherein he hath made us accepted in the beloved" (Eph. 1:6 KJV).

But why are there social and spiritual stigmas in the first place? What are the roots of this obsession with health and fitness? We will seek the answers to these questions in the next chapter.

CHAPTER 5

The Seduction of the Sick

Have We Embraced a Pagan Value?

FIVE HUNDRED YEARS BEFORE THE birth of Christ, another "miraculous" birth took place in the far western border of the then-settled world, a birth that would largely determine the kind of world into which Christ would come—and into which we have come. At a time when the mighty civilizations of the ancient world lay smoldering in ruins, the little town of Athens gave birth to the Greek civilization.

The "Greek miracle" was unlike any civilization before or after it. "In all history, nothing is so surprising or so difficult to account for as the sudden rise of the civilization in Greece."[1] This cultural prodigy seemed to emerge from the womb of history full grown and fully developed, with achievements in art and architecture, in poetry and prose, that have never been surpassed and rarely equaled. The great works they produced are still the standard by which others are judged.

The Greeks perfected the alphabet into a script, which in its Roman form has satisfied the Western world to this day. They invented mathematics and science and philosophy. Thucydides and Xenophon were the first to write history as literature as opposed to mere annals. Deductive reasoning from general premises was a Greek innovation. Never in known history has so much genius in so many areas of human activity been concentrated in one place in such a short period of time.[2]

One of the most significant Greek contributions was a new spirit of inquiry, epitomized by Socrates' precept, "Know thyself." Without any spiritual or intellectual fetters, the Greeks, speculated freely about the nature of the world and the ends of life, raising with artistic precision all the basic questions about human existence. Plato's *Dialogues*, written in the golden days of the Greek civilization, to this day comprise the most influential body of philosophy in the Western world.

So what? What does this have to do with us? And what does it have to do with faith in the midst of sickness, suffering, and death? Just this: We are the inheritors of that Greek culture.

Our Cultural Roots

Our cultural roots go back to the Greeks—Western civilization grew out of that classical world. The flesh and blood of the twenty-first-century Western world hangs on the skeletal system of that ancient culture. As the French Romantic painter Delacroix said, "We are all Greeks." Wayne Meeks writes, "The town of Athens, in the fifth and fourth centuries BC, to an astonishing degree created the categories that Western thinkers would use to talk about ethics from that time until our own."[3]

Our culture has "made in Greece" stamped on it. We think and act differently today because of what the Greeks did in Athens twenty-five hundred years ago.

So what?

Just this: The Greeks created their gods in their own image.

This was something new. Before the Greeks came along, idols bore no resemblance to reality. Remember the pictures of Egyptian gods in your high school history books? They were weird, nightmarish, inhuman: statues with the body of a human and the head of an animal, gods worshipped in the guise of animals. Hathor, for example, was a cow with a woman's head; Montu had the head of a falcon; Anubis, the head of a jackal; and Sekhmet, the head of a lion. The goddess Isis Thoth was sometimes portrayed as a beetle pushing a ball of animal dung mixed with sand. That would make you sing "Hallelujah," wouldn't it?

For the Greeks, man became the measure of all things. Their gods had human form; they looked like men and behaved like men; each had the body and carriage of perfect mortal athletes.

"With the coming forward of Greece," writes Edith Hamilton, "mankind became the center of the universe, the most important thing in it. . . . In Greece alone in the ancient world were people preoccupied with the visible; they were finding the satisfaction of their desires in what was actually in the world around them . . . [their] deities were exceedingly and humanly attractive. In the form of lovely youths and maidens they peopled the woodland, the forest, the rivers, the seas, in harmony with the fair earth and the bright waters."[4]

For Christians, history is *his story*, the record of God's saving purpose on earth, the chronicle of the invisible war between God and Satan, the drama of redemption. History is a single story, belonging to God. But Greek history regards man in control of the affairs of the world. History for the Greeks was not God's story, not the record of the wrath and mercy of God; it was the story of great deeds by great men. And according to historian Oswyn Murray, the Greek tradition has been our tradition. "The Greeks indeed taught the West how *to create and write history without God.*"[5]

They rejected any transcendent frame of reference. Teaching man's superiority over himself, they believed that the finality of truth and good lay within the boundaries of man's own reason. "Know *thyself,*" Socrates said—not, "Know your God." Their morals were derived from human nature, independent of the mind and being of God. They deified nature, treating whatever was natural as divine.

Descendants of Gods and Heroes

To the Greeks, man was not a sinful being in need of redemption. On the contrary, he was the descendent of gods and heroes, and in Greek art his actions and aspirations were performed by the figures of these gods and heroes. They excelled in strength and skill; they lived life with sensual gusto.

The religion of the Greeks was practical and this—worldly. Plato, in his *Dialogues*, said, "For it is and will be the best things ever said, that useful is beautiful and the harmful is ugly. . . . We shall make marriages as sacred as ever we can *and sacred would mean the most useful*" (emphasis added). There were few expressions of interest or concern for a world beyond this one. For them, nothing of value persisted beyond the grave.

Thus it is not surprising to learn that in Greek society a well-developed body was admired (like I said, "We are all Greeks"). In art the images were mostly of the male body, and usually nude. Athletes exercised naked, and the nude bodies of young men were a common sight. Plato argued that the only thing standing in the way of total equality between men and women was the modesty of the woman, and this could be overcome by men and women exercising together unclothed.

Make no mistake about it, the Greeks were pagans, but they were sophisticated pagans whose religion was the cult of youth, health, and beauty. Plato, this time in his *Utopia*, declared that a people living according to the regimen of his ideal state would have no need of doctors. And regarding youth and the aging, Euripides said,

> With food and drink and magic spells,
> Trying to keep death out of the way.
> Since they're no use to the world, they should
> Clear off and leave it to the young.

So for the Greeks "the ideals of life were health, beauty (the Greeks had uncommonly high regard for the male physique), respectable wealth, and enjoyment of youth with friends."[6]

These are among the people of whom Paul writes in Rome: "Professing to be wise, they became fools, and exchanged the glory of the incorruptible God for an image in the form of corruptible man, . . . They exchanged the truth of God for a lie, and worshiped and served the creature rather than the Creator, who is blessed forever" (Rom. 1:22–23, 25).

When Paul says that pagans exchanged the truth of God for a lie, he actually says *"the lie."* In the original Greek Text, "lie" carries the definite article. It is not simply "a lie," it is "The Lie"—The Big Lie.

It's important to recognize that these people were not *deceived by* the lie. They deliberately *chose* it. They knew God but exchanged him for an imitation. If they had not known the true God, idolatry would have been an invention; instead it was a revision. They did not worship idols because they were ignorant; they worshipped idols because they were wicked.

Emphasis on Health a Pagan Value

In this case whatever is natural and beautiful and pleasurable is divine. If it feels good, do it. This is the god to be praised, the goal to be pursued, the good to be possessed.

This is the Big Lie—the idol made in our own image.

So what?

Just this: The present exaggerated emphasis on health, wealth, and happiness is not new, nor is it biblical. Many of the values exalted in our "Christian" culture are pagan in origin. The fact is, we have baptized many pagan values into the church and made them members in good standing. We have, for example, declared physical and material prosperity synonymous with the real Christian life. Oxford historian Jasper Griffin points to the modern cult of athletes and the revival of the Olympic Games as an evidence of the strong influence Greek culture still exercises in our world.[7] Behind the faces of the latest fads are the old gods secular man has worshipped in one form or another for two thousand years. All this is important for our study. J. I. Packer says, "We have grown health conscious in a way that is itself rather sick, and certainly has no precedent—not even in ancient Sparta where physical culture was everything."[8]

The result of all this is "the seduction of the sick." Believing that physical well-being is the Olympic gold of life, we have been seduced into thinking that prosperity is our divine right, that freedom from all woe is God's divine will. The sick are seduced when they are persuaded that prosperity—health, wealth, and happiness—is the highest possible good, that it is something owed them, something God wants them to have above all else. If they push the right buttons, they can escape all evil—evil being anything that interferes with either the existence of, or the full enjoyment of, prosperity. And of course, if they don't have this, their spirituality is in serious doubt. They become pariahs to themselves and to others.

The current distorted emphasis on health and wealth is pagan, not Christian. J. I. Packer dubs it "Hot Tub Religion." The ends of hot tub religion and the world are the same; only the methods are different—the world seeks its prosperity by hook or by crook; the Christian, by faith and prayer. Prosperity religion allows Christians to join the world in its carnal pursuits with a clear conscience, and in the name of God.

Packer observes, "We have recast Christianity into a mold that stresses happiness above holiness, blessings here above blessedness hereafter, health and wealth as God's best gifts, and death, especially early death, not as a thank-worthy deliverance from the miseries of a sinful world, but as the supreme disaster, and a constant challenge to faith in God's goodness."[9]

The seduction of the sick succeeds in large part because the power of faith to obtain health and wealth is preached as a rediscovery of something the church once possessed and practiced, but has long since abandoned. Only now, and only by those with the courage to break free from the fetters of traditionalism, has the "truth" been restored to the church.

The strategy is familiar: The church is made the villain in this melodrama. Eric Hoffer observed that "movements do not usually rise until the prevailing order has been discredited. The discrediting is not an automatic result of blunders and abuses of those in power, but the deliberate work of men of words with a grievance."[10]

Which brings us to this fact: There can be no seduction of the sick without seducers and those willing to be seduced. Have you, or someone you know, embraced their gospel? Have you unwittingly spread their message yourself?

CHAPTER 6

The Seducers

All Seduction Is in Fact Self-Seduction

HAVE YOU EVER LISTENED TO a speaker on radio or TV and only later realized you have been manipulated? That you had bought into an argument that twenty-four hours later seemed highly implausible? You are not alone.

Turn on your TV and watch Dr. Phil, listen to the radio, pick up a newspaper and read "Dear Abby," "Dr. Brothers," and all the other psychologists, physicians, lawyers, and self-proclaimed psychics. Go to the bookstore and wade through the endless shelves of How-to-Do-Everything books, and you'll agree: We are living in the Advice Age. The more forcefully and authoritatively the advice is presented, the more this generation likes it.

Not since the days of Pericles and Socrates, when oratory and rhetoric reigned supreme, have we lived in such a persuasive, manipulative society. Advances in both the techniques of manipulation and in the technology of communication have created a lethal combination that threatens our ability to reason and our capacity to choose.[1] Using state-of-the-art communication and fine-tuned manipulation, the seducer's message has become a massage, creating supposed needs, artificial appetites, controlled desires, and confused values.

Some health-and-prosperity teachers seem more concerned with atmosphere than with accuracy. Persuasion, not precision, is the goal. Through a din of words, slogans, and catchphrases, deriding the "establishment," they exploit the frustrations of the uncured.

"Have the doctors cured you?"

"No."

"Has the church healed you?"

"No."

The message is most compelling on TV. Unfortunately we have anointed TV with an oracular quality, an aura of omniscience and infallibility. According to Harvey Cox of Harvard Divinity School, the mere fact that the preacher is on TV means that his "utterance—any utterance—constitutes a kind of validation of its claims to truth, a psychological reinforcement of a kind understood all too well by demagogues and advertisers."[2]

The prophets of prosperity realized early on the potential of TV and harnessed this new power to voice their special message, becoming experts in communication and persuasion. Cox goes on to say,

> TV reaches us at a level of consciousness below the crucially centered intelligence. . . . The technology of mass media is "one way." It makes us all quiescent consumers of their images and values. . . . People are encouraged by the present technology of media to be "listeners" and "watchers," consumers, not creators. . . . But the process is one of seduction. Genuine human needs are exploited for purposes

foreign to the fulfillment of the viewer. . . . People are not just informed and entertained by them (mass media). They soon begin gauging the significance, and in some sense even the reality, of events on the basis of whether they see them in a magazine or on TV. . . . People begin to distrust their own ideas and impulses if they are not corroborated by the media. . . . The signals begin to prescribe not only what is good and true, but what is real.[3]

A Misplaced Faith

Many who lead sick persons into false expectations and misplaced faith do so unintentionally. They believe what they teach; they are sincere and mean well. Others are less so.

The great seducers of history all had one thing in common: they could use the natural needs and instincts of another person for their own selfish ends. Seducers employ the language and gesture of dialogue, trust, intimacy and personal rapport with consummate skill. They do it, however, not to develop personal intimacy but to subvert it, not to nourish human community but to undermine it. Seduction is the most callous form of exploitation because it tricks the victim into becoming an unwitting accomplice in his own deception.[4]

Well-meaning followers often attribute magical powers to the leader. He appeals to the longing for certainty that is in all of us. He is a simplifier. He *knows*, and knows absolutely, admitting no doubt. He speaks for God; the Lord's words are in his mouth. He leads by slogans and promises. Although I don't agree with much of what Sigmund Freud espoused, I believe he was on the mark when he wrote, "Reasons and arguments are incapable of combating certain words and formulas. They are uttered with solemnity in the presence of groups, and as soon as they have been pronounced an expression of respect is visible on every countenance, and all heads are bowed. By many they are considered as natural forces or as supernatural powers."[5]

Another phenomenon of the seduction of the sick is that it is nearly impossible for the leader to be discredited. His or her followers confer upon their leader a guru infallibility that readily excuses inconsistencies such as adultery or fraud. The leader may publicly declare a well-known religious leader healed of cancer, but when the "healed" man dies, ready explanations, no matter how fantastic or inconsistent, are given and accepted, leaving the leader's credibility miraculously intact. Years ago a televangelist was caught a second time with a prostitute. But the repeat offender, having exhausted all rational explanations the first time around, this time simply stated, "The Lord told me it was none of your business."

It works like this: If you break the spell and cast off the leader, you must give up the dream, the dream of never being sick, of never being without, the dream of prosperity. To keep the dream alive, followers must have their leaders.

But why are we so easily seduced by the promise of these preachers? And why do we continue to follow them after they are discredited? These questions can be answered only when we recognize the universal predisposition to seduction that lies in the human heart. Adam has always been quick to believe a lie. Our capacity for self-deception is mind-boggling. Demosthenes said it all: "Nothing is easier than self-deceit. For what each man wishes, that he also believes to be true."

All Seduction Is Self-Seduction

Like hypnosis, all seduction is in fact self-seduction. We cannot be seduced without our cooperation, however unconscious it may be. The words of Paul Tillich are hard but insightful:

> All people desire false prophets, who, through the glorifications of their gods, glorify their followers and themselves. People long to be flattered in regard to their desires and virtues, their religious feeling and social activity, their will to power and utopian hopes, their knowledge and love, their family and race, their class and nation. And a false prophet can always be found to glorify the demon they worship.[6]

In short, *every god has its guru.*

It is not that these leaders bring out anything new in people. That is not the secret of their success. It is generally agreed that Freud was right when he said, "The greater part of our daily actions are the results of hidden motives which escape our observation."[7] The health-and-wealth teachers are successful because their message appeals to these "hidden" motives. They promise to satisfy the deep-seated longings that we all carry within us—the longing to be free from pain and misery, to escape death and disaster, the longing to have happiness guaranteed, assured, nailed down, in the bag. Larry Crabb gives us insight with these words: "The gospel of health and wealth speaks to our legitimate longing for relief by skipping over the call to endure suffering. . . . *Yet there is no escape from an aching soul, only denial of it*" (emphasis added).[8]

The world is a scary place, filled with a billion dangers. If we knew how close we come to death every day, we would probably go insane. As a matter of fact, it has been suggested that insane people are the ones who see things as they really are and collapse under the load of reality. Perhaps they are the truly sane. Psychologist Otto Rank "used the term 'neurotic' for one type of people who were without illusion, who saw things as they were, who were overwhelmeled by the fragility of the human enterprise."[9]

For some, escaping into health-and-wealth teaching is a part of this protective activity.

This "conspiracy of pretense," in which all of us to one degree or another participate, is called by different names: "life-lies," "vital lie," "life-illusion," or "reality-evasion," which means simply that we have certain ways of evading intolerable and unpleasant aspects of reality. We live in a world created by our own fears and desires; this "life-lie" is the necessary cushion that keeps the jagged edges of life from slashing us. We convince ourselves that things are not really as bad as they seem, that we are more satisfied than we really are, that we are not hurt as deeply as we are, that we have no pain. We deny reality and call it faith because we cannot bear too much truth about our world. We keep the world at bay by our life-lie.

Unfortunately, much in contemporary Christianity contributes to and shores up this life-lie. I was brought up in a very conservative church under a dynamic pastor who preached a great deal on the second coming of Christ. We were taught that all the necessary prophecies had been fulfilled and that Jesus could return at any moment. My pastor avowed again and again that the coming of Christ was so imminent, he believed he would be alive at the Rapture. Well, I was much younger than he, so if he was going to be around for the big show, so would I.

A Way of Escaping Reality

Without realizing it, my belief in the imminent return of Christ became for me more than a theological conviction. It was a way of escaping reality and evading responsibility. There was no need to study hard because Christ would more than likely return before I graduated. What a waste that would be—all that studying! I was happy to believe this. It was unnecessary to plan for retirement and old age because of what was on the verge of happening. There was no need to involve myself in social concerns, no need to clutter my mind with what was happening in the world. In the words of Van B. Weigel, I found myself "reclining on Armageddon's bleachers to await the big event."[10]

All this is summed up by the writer of Hebrews. Describing the death of Christ, the writer says, "Since the children share in flesh and blood, He Himself likewise also partook of the same, that through death He might render powerless him who had the power of death, that is, the devil, and might free those who through fear of death were subject to slavery all their lives" (Heb. 2:14–15). Notice carefully that here it is not death itself that enslaves man—it is the *fear* of death, the dread and terror of it.

In the garden God said to Adam, "From the tree of the knowledge of good and evil you shall not eat, for in the day that you eat from it you will surely die" (Gen. 2:17). But having never seen death, Adam could not know what death was. That was part of the knowledge he gained when he disobeyed God and ate of the tree. He ate to gain knowledge, and the knowledge he gained ate him up, filling him with terror. Now he *knew* (too late) what death was and that he could not escape it. Adam learned death as God slew an animal, as for the first time man witnessed the spectacle of spilled blood, as God wrapped death around man's nakedness. For the rest of his life Adam wore death like a garment.

And so do we. The punishment for man's sin is not merely death but the *knowledge* of it. Of all the creatures of God, only humans know that they will die. And that is the horrendous judgment: Throughout the living of our life, we know we are doomed. In light of that dreadful fact, what else matters but to escape it—at least postpone it? The fear of death "haunts the human animal like nothing else; it is the mainspring of human activity—activity designed largely to avoid the fatality of death, to overcome it by denying in some way that it is the final destiny of man."[11]

There is no mystery why multitudes are seduced by the gospel of health and prosperity. If you drop a lighted match into the gas tank of your car, people will run for cover. Why? Because there is something inside the tank that responds explosively to fire. You wouldn't get the same reaction if you dropped the match into a tank of water. The match is only dangerous when there is fuel in the tank. And there is plenty of fuel in the tank of the human heart to make prosperity teaching powerfully attractive and to make possible the seduction of the sick.

Why are Christians who read the Bible and pray regularly so often no better judges of seduction than the non-Christian? Why can we not discern truth for ourselves when we have the Holy Spirit ready to interpret God's Word for us? A key reason is that we've never learned the principles that help us compare Scripture with Scripture—and Scripture with what the seducers are telling us.

When I was in seminary, I took a course on interpreting the Bible. There's a theological term for this: *hermeneutics*, the rules of interpretation. Usually only preachers and teachers are taught these principles. But if we are to handle accurately the word of truth as the Scriptures admonish, we need these tools. I believe they ought to be available for every Christian so we can interpret the Bible for *ourselves*. This is especially true when we are asking the question, "Will God heal me?"

It's when we are sick that we are often bombarded with countless verses by preachers, teachers, and well-meaning friends. Yet you don't have to be dependent on anyone to tell you what is correct and what is incorrect. With the simple rules of biblical interpretation I will provide in the next chapters, you can do that for yourself. You can know when someone is misrepresenting what the Bible says, especially in the area of health and prosperity. More important, an accurate handling of God's Word will encourage you to set aside the pat, easy platitudes that too often end in disappointment and confusion. You will be able to discover and embrace the more significant purpose of our loving sovereign God in your life. To that end, let's journey onward.

PART TWO

Handling Accurately the Word of Truth

There is no folly, no God-dishonoring theology, no iniquity,
no sacerdotal puerility for which chapter and verse may not
be cited by an enslaved intelligence.
—Edward White, *Inspiration*

Be diligent to present yourself approved to God as a
workman who does not need to be ashamed, accurately
handling the word of truth.
—2 Timothy 2:15

CHAPTER 7

What Do We Mean by "Healing"?

An Important Definition of Terms

I'M SURE SOME OF YOU are asking yourselves what we mean by the term "healing." Are there various kinds or degrees of healing?

Let me try to explain the different terms I use to describe healing. It's a list I developed strictly for the purposes of this book. I do not claim that it is medically exhaustive or scientifically satisfying.

Various Types of Healing

All healing, of course, comes from God. Whether through medication or surgery, proper diet and exercise, alternative medicine, or divine intervention, the body receives its healing from the Lord who created it. The famous French surgeon Ambroise Pare said, "I apply the dressing, but God heals the wound."[1] Hanging on the wall of one doctor's office was the quip: "God does the healing. I charge the fee."

Assisted Healing

This is healing that requires some form of aid, whether medical treatment or therapy, change of diet, or taking two aspirin and going to bed. Nothing in the Bible discourages us from seeking qualified medical help. Luke was a "beloved physician" (either he was very good or he didn't charge much), and Timothy was advised to take a little wine for his stomach (see 1 Tim. 5:23). J. Sidlow Baxter makes an excellent comment on this:

> We may take it as settled that even our infinite God never does the superfluous. He will not intervene to work a miracle where human medication or contrivance can effectively meet the need. I believe that Christians praying for healing should go hand in hand with the human physician or surgeon when the required answer can come that way just as much as we should pray when healing is sought from some malady which is beyond human skill to heal.[2]

Some seek healing, not because their problem is terminal or debilitating, but to avoid the inconvenience of surgery or other medical treatment. To imply that this kind of healing is in the atonement (i.e., Christ died for our sickness as much as for our sin) demeans the cross. Christ did not die to save us from "the heartbreak of psoriasis."

Truth is truth, and all truth, all gifts, "every good thing given and every perfect gift is from above, coming down from the Father of lights" (James 1:17). Whether the physician recognizes it or not, the knowledge, the skill, the truth that enable him to remove a mole or transplant a heart come from God. It is not a lack of faith that sends us to a doctor; we are simply taking advantage of good gifts from God. Faith does not excuse us from the fellowship of human suffering, nor is healing intended to be a substitute for discipline or a crutch for the lazy. God does the healing, but he often uses natural, rather than supernatural, means.

Natural Healing

By this I mean the body's ability to heal itself. Out of the dust of the earth God has fashioned a wonder-filled instrument with amazing recuperative powers. Dr. Andrew Weil says, "Even when treatments are applied with successful outcomes, those outcomes represent activation of intrinsic healing mechanisms which, under other circumstances, might operate without any outside stimulus."[3] We take it so for granted that we fail to wonder at it—this body, as it heals itself of cuts and bruises and sore throats. Often by merely correcting our lifestyle and eliminating harmful habits, the body can heal itself. The body has remarkable recuperative powers, such as when you stop smoking or overeating, it may actually repair damage done.

Lewis Thomas tells of a hunch he had about his fellow doctors and their families. His personal, soft-based, and admittedly unscientific survey found that doctors and their families make less use of medicine and medical help than does the general public. He concludes, "The great secret, known to internists and learned early in marriage by internists' wives, but still hidden from the general public, is that most things get better by themselves. Most things, in fact, are better by morning."[4]

Faith Healing

By "faith" here I do not mean biblical or spiritual faith, our faith in God. I refer to natural faith, the faith that is native to our nature, the faith we exercise when we sit in a chair or fly in an airplane, the power of the mind to influence the body—the power of a positive mental attitude. By "faith healing" I mean believing that if we maintain a positive confession and positive attitude, we will get better.

There's no doubt the state of the mind and the tilt of the attitude play a decisive role in the healing process. "As he thinketh in his heart, so is he" (Prov. 23:7 KJV). And a great many miracles of healing are in truth "faith healings" that are neither miraculous nor divine. With many functional disorders (see chapter 13) it is possible to think yourself well, just as it is possible to think yourself sick. This kind of faith affects the adrenal cortex and increases the effectiveness of the body's immune system. This is not particularly miraculous or supernatural—it is simply mind over matter.

Physicians agree that positive mental thinking results in definite improvement. Cancer specialists continue to see statistical evidence that those patients who believe they will do well with certain treatments have a much better prognosis than those who are pessimistic about their chances for a cure.

All doctors have seen cases of *hysterical blindness* and *hysterical seizures*, maladies whose symptoms appeared only because the patients thought they were sick, or maladies brought on by marked stress resulting in a functional disorder of the body. When someone suffers a severe loss, for example, their grief, if prolonged, can develop into clinical depression.

Many diseases, once thought to be purely physical or organic, are now known to be caused by or related to a person's mental condition. Wade Boggs, therefore, can write, "Thus the methods of faith healers might conceivably be instrumental in curing diseases that have been caused by mental or spiritual conditions. If the faith healer, by means of self-advertising campaigns, can build up an impressive reputation so that his claims are believed by a highly 'suggestible' patient, it is possible that a cure will result."[5]

Physicians have used this type of approach for years by giving "fake medicine," which they have labeled "placebos." Placebo medication has no actual value to the patient other than that the patient believes it will work and therefore begins to relax, confident that healing is in progress. This reassurance mentally conditions the patient to believe that he is better and may actually allow the body's own biochemistry to "regroup," permitting adrenaline levels to go down. By allowing the patient to relax, the body has a chance to unwind itself and begin to function properly.

Divine Healing

For our present purpose, divine healing is defined as the sovereign act of God in which he intervenes to heal the body without the use of human skills or means.

Verifying Divine Healing

When Jesus healed someone, there was no question a miracle had taken place. This is not true with many "miracles of healing" today. When someone we've never seen before and most likely will never see again appears on TV to claim they have been healed of terminal cancer, spectators cannot be blamed for entertaining doubts when they know of many more, perhaps themselves included, who have not been healed.

Unfortunately, questions concerning the validity of a healing miracle are often dismissed as a lack of faith and a hindrance to the Spirit's work. But if we are asked to believe a miracle of healing has occurred, the burden of proof is upon the healer and the healed. Jesus never shielded his patients from inquiry or scrutiny.

Asking for verification is not a sign for unbelief. Truth does not fear investigation.

J. Sidlow Baxter, who believes in divine healing and was an admirer of faith healer Kathryn Kuhlman, says that even though God does heal, we need to weed out the false from the true. He offers the following criteria:

1. The disease or injury must be of sufficient seriousness and duration, either organic or structure (not merely functional), and professionally diagnosed by fully qualified doctors so as to exclude all possibility of exaggeration or deception as to the patient's condition.

2. The healing must be instantaneous or in rapidly connected sequences and of such an abnormal nature as to put it beyond autosuggestions, hypnotism, personal magnetism, or other natural explanations.

3. The healing must be admitted, or better still, verified by fully qualified doctors, including the patient's own private physician, following a fully documented case history.

4. The healing must be further verifiable after a long enough period of time to demonstrate conclusively that it was no mere remission or temporary psychosomatic reversion.[6]

There are various kinds of healing available to the sick person, even direct divine healing. So the sick believer must always stand in hope, believing God for the best. Such healing does not need to fear questions and testing.

CHAPTER 8

Handling Accurately the Word of Truth

Careful, Thorough Bible Study Is Vital to a Faith That Truly Honors God

WE'VE DISCUSSED THE EASE WITH which many Christians are seduced by the doctrine of health and prosperity. We've asked ourselves why that happens. Most important, we've considered how we can counteract the blandishments of the "You can't be sick if you are a Christian" crowd. The question remains: When are we truly hearing the voice of God?

In Arkansas where I grew up, a lot of people consider "hog calling" a fine art. It's true that farmers don't do it much anymore, but hog-calling contests are still staged every year. For miles around you can hear the echoes bouncing from one valley to another: "Woo pig! Sooie! Woooooo pig!" And should you be within ten miles of a University of Arkansas football game, you might hear rapid-fire hog calls from thousands of fans jumping up in the stands, their heads adorned with bright-red plastic hats shaped like a running razorback: "Woo pig! Sooie!" They are cheering their team, the Arkansas Razorbacks, a razorback being a skinny, long-legged, half-wild mongrel hog with a bad disposition.

Once upon a time, according to local lore, an Arkansas pig farmer lost his voice, which not only eliminated him from the annual contest, but made it impossible to call his hogs at feeding time. But he was an inventive fellow and solved the problem by training his pigs to respond to the sound of a stick hitting a tree. Every day at feeding time he would beat on a tree with a stick, and the obedient oinkers would abandon their mud holes and crowd around the feeding trough.

One day the farmer went out to feed his hogs and found them running back and forth, grunting and oinking, lathered in sweat, laboring to get from one tree to another. Several pigs had collapsed in a heap. It took the farmer only a minute to discover what had happened. A flock of woodpeckers had descended upon the farm and were hammering away at the trees, and the porkers were chasing the sounds of the pecking, running from tree to tree, looking for food that wasn't there.

I have doubts about the accuracy of that story but none about the truth it illustrates. Many Christians behave like those unfortunate creatures, confused and frustrated, exhausting themselves scurrying from one voice to another, searching for food that isn't there. And, frankly, some of the voices are like those woodpeckers, pecking on hollow logs.

On a recent Sunday morning as I dressed for church, I flipped on the TV to see what the competition was up to. I watched one minister charge his congregation to adopt a policy of "downward mobility." Instead of accumulating more and more, they should disaccumulate. In light of world hunger, he said, Christians ought to be giving their money to buy food for starving children, rather than buying newer automobiles and large houses and building bigger bank accounts. His listeners were silent and restless—the message was clearly not going over well.

I switched channels and found another minister proclaiming that "prosperity is our divine right," and that God wants us all to be healthy and wealthy. His listeners were shouting "Praise the Lord" and clapping their hands in ecstasy.

No wonder people are confused—especially when it comes to sickness, suffering, and healing. With so many clamoring voices all professing to speak the truth, how can we know what the Bible really teaches? Is there a way that we can find the truth for ourselves?

A Matter of Diligence

Paul offers some help in 2 Timothy 2:15: "Be diligent to present yourself approved to God as a workman who does not need to be ashamed, accurately handling the word of truth."

Any teaching is only as valid as its biblical foundation. "Accurately handling" translates a Greek word that means to cut along a straight line, to cut a straight road through heavily forested country, country difficult to pass through. It means "to guide the word of truth along a straight path (like a road that goes straight to its goal) so that the traveler may go directly to his destination."[1]

Richard Mayhue writes, "The word was used to describe the work of a priest, who sliced through the sacrificial animals according to divine instructions. It also applied to a farmer cutting a straight furrow, a stonemason quarrying huge rocks so they would fit into the wall of a building, and a tailor or tentmaker, who cut cloth. *The key in every case was precision"* (emphasis added).[2]

Precision requires diligence. "Be diligent," Paul counseled Timothy. "Do your best; be zealous and eager. Take pains, make every effort, and be persistent." Handling accurately the Word of Truth demands serious and hard work. Solid, accurate Bible study is not easy, but it is vital to a faith that truly honors God. There is no room here for careless practitioners of the Word.

Just as conception and birth do not occur simultaneously, truth needs time to incubate. The embryo requires time to develop. Ministers sometimes present a truth "secondhand," without first giving it time to prove itself in their own lives or without taking the time and effort to dig it out of the Word themselves to see if it is really "a truth." Someone has said, "Some preachers are like bad photographs—underdeveloped and overexposed."

Remember the account of the transfiguration? With Jesus on the mountain that day were Peter, James, and John; they alone witnessed the awe-full majesty of that holy gathering. What a story to tell! What a sermon to preach! Yet the Bible says, "As they were coming down from the mountain, He gave them orders not to relate to anyone what they had seen, until the Son of Man rose from the dead" (Mark 9:9). Jesus adopted a policy of restraint and timing and pressed upon his disciples the same policy. He knew that his little band of followers, and the public, lacked the spiritual maturity to appreciate that holy happening. Time and experience were needed before the telling of it could be of spiritual benefit (see 2 Pet. 1:16–18). We, too, quickly turn experience into doctrine.

God Has Spoken, But What Has He Said?

The Bible is the product of revelation and inspiration. God revealed himself to man by his deeds, angelic appearances (to Abraham and Gideon), and through the prophets. The Holy Spirit's inspiration enabled man to record that revelation. And what the Spirit inspired, he continues to illuminate. Illumination by the Holy Spirit is essential to a correct understanding of the Scriptures, while an unsound approach to the Bible thwarts the Spirit's work.

Most of the confusion concerning God's perspective on sickness and healing could be eliminated by following the basic rules of biblical interpretation. Clark Pinnock writes,

> The need for principles of interpretation increases in proportion to the distance which the text is in time and culture from our own. . . . Because Scripture is capable of being twisted and mishandled (2 Pet. 3:15–16; 2 Cor. 2:17), it is imperative to observe rules of a sound hermeneutic. A loose hermeneutic may be a cloak for denial of biblical teaching circuited by perverse interpretation. *An orthodox stand on Scripture is short-circuited by perverse interpretation.* [emphasis added][3]

Before we enter the next several chapters, I plead for understanding and open-mindedness from the reader. I do not wish to be mean or vindictive when I discuss the health-and-wealth movement. I have dear friends and family who adhere to this teaching, and I deeply love and respect my brothers and sisters in Christ who may disagree with me. But, having been through the crucible of suffering myself, and having seen serious, chronic, and sometimes fatal illness grip the lives of many wonderful Christian friends who struggled with the question, "Will God heal me?" I must agree with John R. Stott when he wrote, "We have to have the courage to reject the health-and-wealth gospel. It is a false gospel."[4]

Let me now show you why it is false, and most importantly, why a loving God actually allows the travails of sickness, suffering, and death to cross our paths.

CHAPTER 9

Cutting It Straight: Part One

Understanding Three Essential Rules of Biblical Interpretation

OUR FAMILY ONCE HAD A farm in Arkansas (we called it a farm for lack of a better word—we didn't farm it). Several years ago we had a road cut straight back from the lake to the end of our property—about a mile and a half of heavily wooded land. A few days before the bulldozers arrived, my brother and I tied strips of red cloth to certain trees to mark the path of the road-to-be. The red flags were guidelines that enabled the bulldozers to cut a straight path through the woods and arrive at the correct destination.

Remember 2 Timothy 2:15 where Paul charges young Timothy to handle accurately the word of truth? We saw that the phrase "accurately handling" translates a Greek word that means to cut along a straight line, to cut a straight road through heavily forested country. In a real sense, that's what my brother and I were doing.

The rules of interpretation are red flags to guide us through the Scriptures and to keep us on a straight path to the right interpretation of the Word of Truth. Think of these rules as *guidelines*.

Rule #1. God has revealed himself to humankind, and the Bible is the record of that revelation. The Bible, therefore, as the Word of God, is our only guide and absolute authority.

When I was a teenager, there was a popular novelty song called "It's in the Book!" Those words were repeated over and over. Before long everybody was going around saying, "It's in the Book! It's in the Book!"

If we accept the Bible as *soles fidei regula*, the authoritative word from God to man, the question we must ask of every doctrine and of every shade of teaching is, "Is it in the Book?" The full and final revelation of God is recorded in the Bible; there is no authoritative revelation apart from, or outside of, that Word. What many people announce as revelation at best is illumination. Even then, everything must square with what is written in the Bible. The last word on any doctrinal matter is not an experience, observation, or feeling—or even a word of prophecy from modern prophets—it is only the last word if it is clearly taught in the Bible.

I cannot overstate the importance of this first principle. Like buttoning your shirt, if you get the first button in the wrong buttonhole, you're going to be off all the way. This principle is the "first button" in the process of correctly buttoning your shirt.

About now, you may be thinking, "Doesn't everybody accept the Bible as God's final revelation?" Evidently not everyone does, for many are ignoring it. A subtle erosion of this principle is occurring throughout contemporary Christianity. One prominent author wrote that the Holy Spirit has not confined his revelation to the truths contained in the canons of the Old and New Testaments.[1] In other words, the Holy Spirit is giving revelations today that are as valid and inspired as those found in the Bible. Carless teaching like this sets loose all kinds of confusion, misunderstanding, and heresy. It is a license for anyone to claim they are speaking "from the Lord."

The fact is the Holy Spirit has limited revelation to the Old and New Testaments. Jude opens his epistle by writing "Beloved, while I was making every effort to write you about our common salvation, I felt the necessity to write to you appealing that you contend earnestly for the faith which was once for all handed down to the saints" (v. 3).

Note the phrase "once for all delivered to the saints." "The faith" refers to the whole body of Christian truth, the complete revelation of God to man. The definite article, "the," points to the one and only faith." There is no other.

"Once for all" refers to something done for all time, needing no addition or repetition. And the word *delivered* is a Greek participle indicating that it has been completed and stands complete. The word is used for handing down authorized tradition in Israel, and Jude is saying that the apostolic tradition is normative for the people of God.

The Bible is the only objective part of our faith. The rest is subjective and easily misinterpreted. A man in St. Louis actually said to me: "I don't care what the Bible says. I've had an experience." (Surely he didn't intend to say it just like that.)

Peter Donovan was correct when he said, "Religious experience nowadays arouses more public interest than religious doctrine or theology."[2] True, experience is a powerful persuader, but as a reliable interpreter of religious truth it is profoundly inadequate and can be downright misleading.

For one thing, we cannot always accurately interpret our own experience. There is an important difference between "feeling certain" and being right. Nor can we always accurately interpret the experience of someone else. In the Gospel of John, for example, when Jesus prayed that the Father's name would be glorified, a voice answered from heaven. It was his Father's voice saying, "I have both glorified it, and will glorify it again." So the crowd of people who stood by and heard it were saying that it had thundered; others were saying 'An angel has spoken to Him'" (John 12:28–29).

No desire is more natural, more human, than the desire for supernatural knowledge. We try every means that may lead us to it. When reason fails, we make use of experience, which is a feebler and less worthy way. Theologian J. I. Packer writes, "Experience is a slippery word, and *experience* . . . coming to imperfectly sancti- fied sinners cannot but have dross mixed in with their gold. No *experience* just by happening can authenticate itself as sent by God to further His work of grace. The mere fact that a Christian has an experience does not make it a Christian experience."[3]

Packer's last sentence is worth emphasizing: Not every experi- ence a Christian has is necessarily a Christian experience.

The phenomena many Christians claim as their special experience have also been experienced by non-Christians. For example, people both inside and outside the Christian faith report out-of-body death experiences. Anthropologists know that among primitive pagan tribes similar incidents have occurred: priests speaking in unknown tongues, visions, prophetic utterances, physical healing, casting out contrary spirits. This doesn't mean that all similar Christian experience is false—it means that such experiences cannot authenticate themselves.

And then there is the inclination to make our experience a standard for everyone else. If God healed me, that means he will heal you. If God made me wealthy, that means he wants all of his children to be wealthy. Let God do something extraordinary for one person, and we rush to declare it an ordinary experience for every Christian.

We are told, for example: "If God did it for the apostles, he will surely do it for us." But church doctrine is not based on the apostles' experiences—it is based on their *teaching*. Paul had a dramatic conversion experience on the road to Damascus, but it would be foolish to demand that every genuine conversion happen exactly like that.

The ultimate danger of making human experience more important than Scripture is turning what we learn from experience into doctrine. For example, if God heals a thousand people of terminal cancer, it means only one thing: God healed one thousand people of cancer. It does not necessarily mean he will do the same for you or me.

A More Subtle Danger

Another danger we must avoid is "deductive doctrines": making a logical deduction from a biblical truth and treating the conclusion we reach as biblical truth.

One example of this "deductive doctrine" approach involves divine healing and the "better covenant" of Hebrews. We are told that in Christ we have a better covenant. This means that if God healed people in the Old Testament days under the old covenant, it only makes sense that God will do no less under the new, better covenant. Our covenant is better; therefore, we have everything they had under the old covenant, plus more. This is reasoning from biblical truth and treating our conclusion as divine revelation, when it is, in fact, human assumption. In his treatment of the better covenant, the author of Hebrews never mentions physical

healing, nor does Jeremiah in his great passage on the new covenant (see Jer. 31:31).

To make such a deduction forces our concept of "better" on
God, and it is always a mistake to assume that God thinks as we
do. His value system is vastly different. With God, spiritual is
better than physical, forgiveness better than healing, assurance
better than wealth.

The Holy Spirit has confined inspired and infallible revelation to the books of the Old and New Testaments. "The function
of the Spirit," writes Bernard Ramm, "is not to communicate new
truth or to instruct in matters unknown, but to illuminate what
is revealed in Scripture."[4]

The Spirit illumines only that which is already written in
Scripture. He gives us the wisdom to know what lies within the
Scripture, not beyond it. It is through his illumination that we
know not only what is written there but how to apply it to our
daily lives.

In the Middle Ages, Hugo of St. Victor recommended an
approach many take today: "Learn first what you should believe,
and then go to the Bible to find it there." Unfortunately, this backward approach is still very much in use. A better rule to follow is
to say no more than the Bible says. Where the Bible is silent, let
us be silent. The Puritan writer John Trapp advised, "Where the
Scripture hath no tongue, we must have no ears." To go further
than the Bible goes is going too far.

Rule #2. The primary theme of revelation is redemption.

The Bible deals with ultimate truth. Writing to Timothy, Paul
says that the purpose of Scripture is to make us wise unto salvation, and he goes on to say, "All Scripture is inspired by God and
profitable for teaching, for reproof, for correction, for training in
righteousness; so that the man of God may be adequate, equipped

for every good work" (2 Tim. 3:16–17). These words remind us that the purpose of Scripture is to evangelize and to edify.

Bernard Ramm states, "'Jesus wants you well' and 'God is committed to your happiness' are themes that in some circles are superseding the biblical call to repentance towards God, faith in the Lord Jesus Christ, and obedience to the leadership of the Holy Spirit."[5]

When I was a boy, a preacher whose specialty was prophecy came to our church for a week of meetings. He had found in some passage of the Old Testament predictions of the tire shortage in World War II, of tanks, of submarines, and flamethrowers. I remember hearing someone say that he was a "deep preacher." But he wasn't deep—he was muddy. Surely God had more important things to talk about. Such fanciful manipulation of God's Word only tickles people's ears. J. Robertson McQuilkin drives home the point:

> To say that salvation is the purpose of Scripture means that revelation is limited. The Bible is not given to teach all there is to know about an infinite God, or about his universe. God did not inspire the biblical writers to provide a definitive record of ancient history or even teach all there is to know about the nature of man. To use the Bible as a textbook on biology, psychology, sociology is to misappropriate Scripture and to undermine its authority.[6]

The Bible is not meant to be a comprehensive handbook on economics, nutrition, or politics. It never professes to contain all truth about all things. Much of that which stirs our imagination and excites our curiosity is untouched by the Scriptures—which is further evidence of its divine authorship. Over three hundred years ago Descartes said, "To want to draw from Sacred Scripture the knowledge of truths which belong solely to the human sciences and have no bearing on salvation is to use Scripture for a purpose for which God did not intend it and consequently to abuse it."

Rule #3. The revelation of God is progressive (or culminant).

Two words provide the key to understanding progressive revelation: *accommodation* and *apprehension*—the accommodation of God to the apprehension of people. When God revealed himself, he spoke in a language humans could understand. You don't talk to a three-year-old the same way you talk to a thirty-year-old, nor does God. When speaking to a child, you accommodate yourself to the child's ability to understand what you are saying. In the Bible we see God bringing humans up through the infancy of the Old Testament to the maturity of the New Testament.

Progressive revelation is humankind's growing comprehension of the redemptive purpose of God that culminated in the coming of Christ. It means that God revealed to us only that which we were able to comprehend. In the infancy of the human race, he led us slowly and carefully, step by step.

Jesus was referring to this when he said, "Do not think that I came to abolish the Law or the Prophets; I did not come to abolish but to fulfill" (Matt. 5:17). He did not come to annul the law, but to bring it from a bud to a blossom. The law was right and good as far as it went, but it did not go far enough or high enough or deep enough. Paul wrote of "the fullness of the time" (Gal. 4:4). The time before Christ was the kindergarten of the human race; with Christ came higher education. In the Old Testament, God was teaching the ABCs; in the New Testament, he is teaching the XYZs. The letter to the Hebrews puts it this way: "God, after He spoke long ago to the fathers in the prophets in many portions and in many ways, in these least days has spoken to us in His Son" (Heb 1:1–2).

The full, final, and complete revelation of God awaited the coming of Christ, and with him all that we will ever need to know about God—at least in this world.

Progressive revelation does not mean extra-biblical revelations. Nor does it mean that God evolved with his creatures, or that he grew less violent and more merciful in the New Testament period.

Nor does it mean that the Old Testament is incorrect or invalid or less inspired than the New Testament. Progressive revelation ("culminant revelation" may be a better term) says that the final revelation is in the New Testament. The Old Testament, therefore, must be read and interpreted in the light of the New. Gerhard von Rad spoke of the "actualization" of the Old Testament in the New, saying that the Old Testament could only be read as a book of ever-increasing anticipation, a book in which expectation mounts with the turning of every page.[7] The Old Testament "leans" toward the New Testament.

What Authority Does the Old Testament Have?

This leaves us with a problem. How should we behave toward the Old Testament? Does it speak with authority to the New Testament Christians? If the Old Testament is not final and complete, if it deals in shadows and symbols, pictures and previews, if it is not the last word, what part applies to us today? Are its commands, codes, and ceremonial laws binding on the church? We can be fairly certain that we aren't to offer animal sacrifices, stone adulterers, or chop off the hands of thieves. But there is much in the Old Testament that is ethically, morally, and spiritually relevant. How do we know what part was for the child and what part is for the adult?

First, let's understand that the Old Testament is indeed relevant for twenty-first-century Christians. It does speak with authority to the church. From the second-century heresy of Marcion (who rejected the Old Testament) to the present, there have been attempts to get rid of the Old Testament, if not as a fact, then as a force in the church. But the New Testament is rooted in the earth of the Old, and neither can exist without the other.

In what way, then, is the Old Testament relevant? Not in its ancient forms and institutions; not in its legal codes and ceremonial rites—those belong to an ancient culture of an ancient world. In his book *The Authority of the Old Testament*, John Bright writes,

> The Old Testament's forms of belief and practice cannot be our forms, or directly a model for them. Indeed, in many of its texts the Old Testament seems in its plain meaning to have little to say to us as Christians. But it is as we examine these ancient forms and ancient texts, lay hold of those theological concerns that inform them, and then see what the New Testament has done with that theology in the light of Christ—it is then, through its theology, that the Old Testament speaks its authoritative word to the Church.[8]

The key word here, I think, is "theology." It is not in the time-bound forms of the Old Testament that we find its relevance and authority, but in the theology of those forms. For example, the sacrificial system of the Old Testament is out-of-date, but not its message—that humans have sinned and atonement must be made.

Here, then, is the rule: Only those words of the Old Testament—the moral, ethical, and religious teachings—that are *reiterated in the New Testament* are relevant and authoritative for the church today.

The New Testament Is Our Guide

Our guide must be the New Testament, the "Christianized" version of the Old. In determining the relevance of an Old Testament word, we ask, "Does this reappear in the New Testament? Is this part of the revelation of God that Christ brought with him into the New Testament, or is it part of that which he left behind because it had served its purpose and was no longer needed? And if the particular form of a word from the Old Testament does appear in the New, has it been redefined?"

The Old Testament, for example, is more physical and material in its approach to salvation; it speaks largely in terms of physical deliverance. The concept of a hereafter, of the eternal, was barely formed in the minds of the Israelites. Righteousness in the Old Testament days was pictured as outward obedience and external observance of rules and rituals.

The prevailing philosophy of that period indicated that physical and material blessings were evidence of God's favor. It was really very simple—if you were right with God you would be healthy and wealthy if you were *not* right with God you would be sick and bankrupt.

No wonder Job's three friends accused him of harboring sin. Warren Wiersbe tells us that Job's plight was a threat to his friends: "His experience challenged the validity of their cut-and-dried theology . . . This meant that what happened to Job *could happen to them*! They were not really interested in Job as a hurting person. Their major concern was in Job as a problem to be solved, not a person to be encouraged."[9] The same philosophy flourishes today.

Recently I received a newsletter from a certain ministry, and the lead article revolved around these words: "Your financial condition is a reflection of your spiritual condition." Would Job agree? What especially fascinated me was that on the same day I received the newsletter, I also received a letter from the head of that ministry. In that letter he was appealing for money because of his ministry's overwhelming debts and needs. Amazing.

My point is that, for those who derive their "You can't be sick or poor and Christian" worldview from the Old Testament, the perspective of the Old Testament differs from that of the New and must be interpreted with this in mind. As Bernard Ramm points out, "Inasmuch as the New Testament is the capstone of revelation, it must be taken as the chief source of biblical doctrine. . . . Therefore, whatever is shadowed in the Old Testament is realized in the New, which in turn makes the New Testament the chief source of Christian theology. The great doctrines of faith . . . are all most clearly developed in the New Testament."[10]

A good example of how the old covenant telescopes into the new can be seen by comparing Habakkuk 2:3 with Hebrews 10:37. Here is shadow becoming substance, the lesser advancing to and being absorbed by the greater. In a time of national emergency, God promised Habakkuk that deliverance would come: "For the vision is yet for the appointed time; it hastens toward the goal and it will not fail. Though it tarries, wait for it; for it will certainly come, it will not delay."

Centuries later, to encourage persecuted believers, the writer of Hebrews quotes Habakkuk, using the *New Covenant Version*: "For yet in a very little while, he who is coming will come, and will not delay."

Notice that Habakkuk writes of *it* coming; Hebrews speaks of *he* who is coming. What is an *it* in the Old Testament is a *he* in the New. Christ is the "Yes" and "Amen" of all God's promises. In him all the promises are filled to the full. This is what is better about the "better covenant" of which Hebrews speaks—*he* is better than *it*.

With that established, it's also important to point out that *interpreting the New Testament in the light of the Old* can be one of the chief causes of confusion about physical healing.

A friend and his wife, who suffered severe migraine headaches, attended a Bible conference led by two well-known ministers. Visiting together one evening after the session, she happened to mention her headaches. The two preachers questioned her at length about her background, her parents, and grandparents. They concluded that the headaches were the result of a curse passed on to her from her mother who had played with a Ouija board as a child, which gave the Devil a point of entry, and which (said curse) obviously had not been broken by her mother. After praying for healing, rebuking the Devil, and renouncing the curse, the preachers advised her to stop taking the medication her doctor had prescribed. This would be her act of faith, her positive confession. Which is how I got involved—her doctor had warned her from the start of the treatment that a sudden withdrawal from the medicine could trigger a cardiac arrest. She asked me what I thought about that. I told her I didn't think much of it and that I'd stay on the medication.

The conference leaders had based their actions on the passages in Deuteronomy 27 and 28, which talk about curses. I pointed out that those words were spoken in a different time-and-space situation from ours, that they were spoken to a specific people, at a specific time, dealing with a specific situation peculiar to Israel at that time. Those verses in Deuteronomy did not apply to Christians today.

Why did I say that? Because no such thing is taught in the New Testament. I ran those verses through the filter of the New Testament and they didn't come out at the other end. You may be thinking about the passage in the fourth chapter of James. There it says something about curses, but both exegetically and grammatically, the "curses" of which James speaks are not even remotely similar to a voodoo-type curse or hex.

I guess what grieves me the most about this incident is that this careless theology endangered the wife of my friend.

Only those teachings of the Old Testament that are reiterated in the New Testament, either in form or theology, apply to us today. Wiersbe makes this observation:

> God promised healing and prosperity to Israel, but He never gave those promises to the New Testament church. . . . They were in the infancy of their nationhood and, like all children, had to learn primarily through rewards and punishments . . . but there comes a time when children must learn to obey, not because obedience is profitable, but because obedience is *right*. They must obey from inward constraint, from love, and not from outward compulsion and fear. . . . People today who urge suffering believers "to have more faith" or to "get right with God" are unconsciously agreeing with Satan and Job's friends. They are asking us to regress into childhood rather than grow into maturity.[11]

Health-and-wealth theology and its excess baggage, such as "curses," drag believers back into the old covenant and the uncertainty of immaturity.

CHAPTER 10

Cutting It Straight: Part Two

How to Correctly Interpret a Specific Bible Passage

NOW THAT WE'VE CONSIDERED THE overarching rules of biblical interpretation, let's examine those more specifically focused on interpreting a particular passage. When these rules are violated, misleading conclusions are reached and often proclaimed as original insight or even as revelation. But when these rules are followed, you'll find that the Bible is consistent within itself on the issues of health and healing.

Rule #4. We must distinguish between the picture and the frame.

Hanging over the fireplace in our home is a beautiful painting illustrating the hymn, "How Firm a Foundation." The hymn has special meaning for Kaye and me. When our oldest son died in

1976, Miss Bertha Smith, a retired missionary from China, called us from her home in Cowpens, South Carolina. When I answered the phone, she asked Kaye to pick up the extension, and then, without another word, she began to sing that great song.

When Japanese planes bombed the hospital she was attached to during World War II, Miss Bertha crawled under some hospital beds, dragging with her several terrified nurses. To calm the nurses and herself, she sang all seven verses of "How Firm a Foundation" over and over. The hymn had been a source of strength in her hour of crisis, and she thought it might be the same for us. It was and still is.

The hymn was painted for us by a gifted young woman in our church who knew of the song's significance to us. Later, when we redecorated the den, we replaced the original frame with one that blended in with the new color and décor of the room. We didn't get a new picture; we got a new frame. The picture is permanent, the frame is temporary.

In much the same way, when God revealed himself to humans, he did so within a specific time frame, an age with particular cultural backgrounds and settings. The Bible is rooted in history. It is a collection of books and letters, not without addresses and dates, thus possessing a historical, geographical, and cultural setting (the frame) in which God placed spiritual and eternal truths (the picture). To put it another way, God dressed eternal truths in period costumes. But he does not expect us to wear the clothes and adopt the customs of that ancient age in which the Bible was given.

When we open the Bible, we are AD (after Christ) people reading BC (before Christ) documents, documents written thousands of years ago in different languages from diverse settings and cultures. It is the Word of God, but it is also a historical document.

Augustine said, "Distinguish the times and you will harmonize Scripture." Our first task in interpreting a passage of Scripture is to discover what it meant to the original readers. We cannot know what it means to us until we know what it meant to them.

Some experts of interpretation call this "distanciation," meaning that, in one sense, we must "distance" ourselves from the text. D. A. Carson says that unless "we recognize the 'distance' that separates us from the text being studied, we will overlook the differences of outlook, vocabulary, interest; and quite unwittingly we will read our mental baggage into the text without pausing to ask if it is appropriate."[1] We will read their words but with our definitions.

For example, Paul wrote to the Corinthians "concerning the eating of things sacrificed to idols" (1 Cor. 8:4). Having been sacrificed on a pagan altar to a pagan god, the remains of the luckless animal would then be sold in the public meat market. In Paul's day eating meat that had been offered to idols was a controversial and hotly debated issue. Frankly, I have no problem with that today; it's a subject that just never comes up. When I go to the Tom Thumb supermarket, I never ask the butcher if the hamburger meat has been sacrificed to idols. The historical situation has little or no relevance in our day. It was simply the frame into which was placed a lasting truth and eternally relevant principle: "But take care that this liberty of yours does not somehow become a stumbling block to the weak" (1 Cor. 8:9).

A few years ago at the Keswick Convention in England, a woman asked me if I thought we ought to obey the Bible. There was only one answer to that.

"Yes, of course," I said.

"Then," she said, the bait having been taken, "why don't we greet the brethren with a holy kiss, like the Bible says?"

I assumed she was referring to Peter's words in 1 Peter 5:14 or one of Paul's admonitions, like Romans 16:16, where we are told to "greet one another with a holy kiss."

"In the first place," I said, "the emphasis in Paul's words are on *holy*, not kiss. In the second place, greeting one another with a kiss was the customary greeting of that day and culture—and still is." I remember seeing Yasser Arafat greet the president of Jordan on TV by kissing him on both cheeks—and the nose. Paul and Peter were not telling their readers to greet one another with a kiss—they were already doing that—but to make sure it was a *holy* kiss. The gesture of kissing, I told the woman, was the same as a handshake for us.

If Paul were writing these words to us, he would probably say, "Greet one another with a holy handshake." The frame is the act of kissing, the picture is a *holy* kiss and, according to 1 Peter 5:14, a *loving* greeting.

Rule #5. Scripture interprets Scripture.

The Bible is its own best interpreter. Every verse must be interpreted in light of its own immediate context as well as in the total context of the Bible. "The unity of the Scripture," writes Clark Pinnock, "follows from the fact that God is the principal Author of it, and implies that the meanings of the parts agree with the meaning of the whole, so that one passage sheds light on another. . . . Because it comes from one Divine Author, Scripture is its own interpreter."[2]

The Bible is a collection of sixty-six books, written by different people separated by hundreds of years. Yet it is one book, possessing one scheme of truth, one consistent theology, in which all the separate parts harmonize with one another.

This is sometimes referred to as the "analogy of faith," which says that there is one and only one system of doctrine taught in the Bible; therefore, the individual interpretation must conform to that one system. "We may define it (analogy of faith) to be the *consistent and perpetual harmony of Scripture in the fundamental points of faith and practice*, deduced from those passages, in which they are discussed by the inspired penmen, either directly or expressly, and in clear, plain and intelligible language" (emphasis added).[3]

The theological unity of the Bible means that the interpretation of a specific passage must not contradict the total teaching of Scripture on a point. As the old maxim goes, "A text without a context is a pretext." Isolating verses from their context is a careless, reckless, and even dangerous way of establishing truth. Everyone is familiar with the classic ludicrous example: "Judas went out and hanged himself . . . Go thou and do likewise. . . . And whatsoever thou doest, do quickly."

Bernard Ramm points out, "It is almost instinctive with conservatives to grant a point in theology if a proof text is given. *But there must be a sound exegetical examination of every text cited* or else we are guilty of superficial treatment of Scripture. The use of proof texts is only as good as the exegesis undergirding the citation" (emphasis added).[4]

This principle, that Scripture interprets Scripture, calls for three considerations:

1. *We must give attention to grammar, the meaning of the words, and their relation to one another within a verse.* Martin Luther's advice deserves mention: "Keep hard at the languages, for language is the sheath in which the sword of the Spirit rests." Theology starts with the grammatical and exegetical foundation that underlies it. Bible study that ignores the meaning of the word and its

relation to other words within that verse is unreliable and careless and should not be regarded as serious study.

2. *Obscure passages must give way to clear passages.* Let's face it—some parts of the Bible are downright difficult to understand. You think you have a hard time understanding Paul? You're in good company, for Peter himself had trouble with some of Paul's writing: "Our beloved brother Paul, according to the wisdom given him, wrote to you, as also in all his letters, speaking in them of these things, *in which are some things hard to understand*" (2 Pet. 3:15–16). But Ramm points out, "Everything essential to salvation and Christian living is clearly revealed in Scripture. Essential truth is not tucked away in some incidental remark in Scripture nor in some passage that remains ambiguous in its meaning even after being subjected to very thorough research."[5]

A teaching that is built upon an obscure passage of Scripture is suspect. For instance, some have devised a doctrine of material and physical prosperity based on John's salutation to Gaius: "Beloved, I pray that in all respects you may prosper and be in good health, just as your soul prospers" (3 John 2).

And some have come away from 1 Peter 2:24 (KJV) with a detailed theology of healing in the atonement by superimposing upon the text something that is not there. The words "by whose stripes ye were healed" are unmistakably metaphorical, referring to the spiritual healing from our sins.

3. *Quoting verses and preaching the Word are not the same thing.* Some teachers bombard their listeners with verse after verse from every corner of the Bible, verses bearing no relation to one another. In these cases, there's rarely an attempt to reconcile one verse with the other or to explain

their exegetical meaning or their contextual significance. The listeners of some health-and-wealth preachers are inundated with hundreds of isolated texts, mostly from the Old Testament, and when New Testament verses are used, their relationship to healing is vague at best. Quoting a steady stream of verses is impressive and can overwhelm an audience. Often scrutiny of the verses is discouraged, and questions concerning the accuracy or relevance of texts quoted are considered irreverent acts of unbelief. As one preacher, after quoting scores of isolated verses, warned his congregation: Don't analyze it—just believe it!"

This is a naïve and shallow view of both faith and preaching, Faith does not fear facts. Truth doesn't resist questions; it welcomes analysis. Merely reciting verses, heaping one on top of the other, is not "preaching the Word."

Matthew 10:1 is a good example of interpreting Scripture out of context: "Jesus summoned His twelve disciples and gave them authority over unclean spirits, to cast them out, and to heal every kind of disease and every kind of sickness." Some use this verse to support the claim that we have the same power and authority Jesus gave his disciples; we can "do the works" of Jesus just as Jesus did them. Since Jesus so clearly commanded his disciples to heal the sick, cast out demons, and raise the dead, we can do the same.

This, of course, is not the case. Jesus goes on to instruct his disciples to go only to the lost sheep of Israel, avoiding the Gentiles and the Samaritans. In verses 9 and 10, Jesus further instructs them that they must not "acquire gold, or silver, or copper for your money belts, or a bag for your journey, or even two coats, or sandals, or a staff; for the worker is worthy of his support." If we lay claim to verse 1, we must also claim the following verses. This would mean that we can minister only to the Jews—no preaching or healing among the Gentiles. We must raise the dead as well as heal the sick; we must not acquire any money, and carry only one suit and one pair of shoes. I have heard many Christians claim verse 1, but I have never heard anyone make the same claim for the verses that follow. If anyone ever set out on the circuit with only one suit and one pair of shoes and did not acquire any gold or silver along the way, I missed him when he came to my town. J. Sidlow Baxter observes,

> The rule of context is powerfully obvious here. That Jesus meant this commission for the original twelve only, and that it was limited to a specific group in a specific time frame is made clear by verse two: "Now the names of the twelve apostles are these . . . ," then Jesus lists them by name . . . Dear brother, if your name is not among the list of the Twelve, the commission was never given to you.[6]

Again, ignoring this rule of interpretation can lead to yet another common error—superimposing Western culture and values upon the Bible. The "doctrine of prosperity," the idea that God wants every Christian to be materially wealthy, is the result of forcing our economic values upon the pages of the Bible.

One religious speaker asserted that Jesus established the "doctrine of prosperity" by riding into Jerusalem on a donkey. Let's pause a moment and let that sink in. Riding on a donkey, he said, was the equivalent of driving a luxurious limousine. Now there's nothing wrong with driving a limousine, but to establish a biblical doctrine on that incident defies reason and slaps common sense in the face. Anyway, the donkey was borrowed. Rather than the doctrine of prosperity, Jesus supposedly established the doctrine of "rent-a-car."

Only an affluent society could beget such a doctrine. Let's face it—where else but in America can you buy low-calorie dog food for overweight canines? Speaking to the idea that God never intends his children to suffer poverty, J. I. Packer says, "The claim may sound plausible when made by a wealthy banker in a luxurious hotel ballroom, but one only has to imagine it being voiced to Christian villages in India or Bangladesh or some drought-ridden part of Africa to see how empty it is."[7]

Rule # 6. We must take into account the literary character of the book.

While the Bible is one book, it is more than one book. It is a collection of books—and a multifaceted collection at that. The full range of literary forms appears in the Scriptures: historical narratives, poetry, proverbs, hymns, allegory, law, prose.

This is a vital factor in understanding the Bible. The approach to each literary style must be different. Interpreting Acts the same way we interpret Ezekiel will lead to no small amount of confusion.

The Psalms are largely poetic writings, filled with vivid images. I seriously doubt God has wings (see Ps. 17:8), and we do not interpret literally these words: "He shall cover thee with his feathers" (Ps. 91:4 KJV).

The four Gospels and the book of Acts are cast largely as historical narratives and this influences our approach to them. Early in my ministry I wondered if churches should meet in homes as they did in the book of Acts; I'd heard others suggest we should. But I suspect the people in Acts may have met in homes because they had no other place to gather. Whatever the reason, we are not instructed to meet in homes. And this is an important point:

Our doctrine comes not from what the apostles did, but from what they taught. Nor does it come from what the apostles experienced, but again from what they taught.

"It is an axiom," writes John Phillips, author of the *Exploring* series of commentaries, "That you don't get your doctrine from the book of Acts."[8]

In one way the Gospels and the Acts present the same question as does the Old Testament: Since they are historical documents, how do we separate the picture from the frame? Much of the Gospel record is clearly universal and eternal in its application, such as the ethical and moral teachings of the Sermon on the Mount, the "upper room" discourse, the truths expressed through the parables, and obviously timeless laws like "Then He said to them, 'Beware, and be on your guard against every form of greed; for not even when one has an abundance does his life consist of his possessions'" (Luke 12:15).

But what about foot-washing? Baptism? Communion? Healing? On matters such as these we turn to the Epistles; here is where church doctrine is established. We interpret the Gospels and the Acts in the light of the Epistles. What teachings, commands, and precepts are reiterated in the Epistles? This is why most churches do not observe foot-washing as an ordinance of the church. There is no evidence the early church practiced it as such, and it is not taught in the Epistles.

Now let's apply this to the question of healing. Do the Epistles teach it? Do they exhort us to claim a divine right to the healing of all our maladies?

In view of the prominent place healing occupies in the Gospels and Acts, we are surprised to find almost nothing about it in the rest of the New Testament. If the church is supposed to believe in and practice apostolic healing, it should be taught in the Epistles. But it is not. Nowhere is it taught or even suggested that we have the divine right to be healed of any or all sickness and maladies. Concerning this, J. Sidlow Baxter says,

> This sparse mention of the subject in the Epis-
> tles strikes a sharp contrast with the frequency of
> miracle healings in the four Gospels and the Acts of
> the Apostles. And let us be reminded, it is the New
> Testament *Epistles*, not the Gospels or the Acts,
> which are specifically addressed to the church as a
> whole, to local churches, and to individual Chris-
> tians as such. It is the Epistles which are exclusively
> the property of the Church and furnish all those
> teachings which are specifically "church" doctrines
> and which reveal all the Lord's special provisions
> for His Church and which set the norm for the
> Church's life, fellowship, witness, and experience
> throughout the present age.[9]

The conclusion seems obvious: If the emphasis of our ministry is to be the same as that of the apostles' teaching, we cannot
justify the excessive accent on physical healing and deliverance or
on material prosperity.

I said at the beginning of these chapters that these principles
of interpretation, while not exhaustive, are basic—and sufficient.
Observing these six guidelines can safeguard us against doctrinal error, enable us to recognize false teaching, and equip us to
handle accurately the word of truth. Now let's apply these rules of
interpretation to the issue of whether Jesus' miracles ought to be
duplicated today by contemporary Christians.

CHAPTER 11

Healing: The Same Yesterday, Today, and Forever?

Are the Miracles of the New Testament Being Repeated Today?

MAYBE YOU'VE HEARD EXPRESSIONS LIKE THESE:

"Bible days are here again!"

"First-century Christianity is being restored to the modern-day church!"

Slogans like these abound today, supported by testimonies of great miracles, especially miracles of healing, and these claims often seem justified. Teaching like this finds ready converts among believers who are spiritually undernourished. Their churches seem dry and dead. Frustrated by the impotence of their own faith, they are eager to believe something new, to see something exciting, to feel something . . . supernatural.

But many of these testimonies are questionable, and much of the theology lacks sure biblical foundation. Not all the "healings" last, and for every person who is healed, a thousand are not.

Are Bible days here again? Are the miracles of the New Testament being repeated today? Have first-century signs and wonders really been restored to the modern-day church? We should not fear a close examination of the facts, for truth is never afraid of investigation—it welcomes it.

At the heart of the healing debate are the miraculous healings performed by Jesus and his disciples. Many insist that what happened during New Testament days should be the standard for our day and for every church age. If Jesus and his followers did these things, then we may also—if we believe.

The best way to resolve the issue is to compare the healing miracles of the New Testament with those of today. Are we seeing the same signs and wonders? (See rule 3 of biblical interpretation in chapter 9.)

I'm not implying that God must heal today as he did then. God cannot be boxed in with any one method; he can heal any way he chooses.

The issue is not merely whether God heals today, but whether the earthly ministry of Jesus and the apostles has been restored to modern Christianity. Does God intend that ministry to be reproduced today? Is he imparting to present-day believers the same miraculous ministry exercised by Jesus and his apostles? If so, there should be an obvious similarity between yesterday's ministry and today's.

In this chapter let's first examine two of the primary texts used most often to support atonement healing (the belief that Christ died for our sicknesses as well as for our sins) in John 14:12 and Hebrews 13:8.

The Greater Works of John 14:12

In John 14:12 we read that Jesus told his disciples, "Truly, truly, I say to you, he who believes in Me, the works that I do, he will do also; and greater works than these he will do; because I go to the Father." This is a fantastic promise, and the phrase "he who believes in Me" extends the promise beyond the immediate disciples. It is made to anyone "who believes in Me," and that includes us.

Admittedly, at first glance this verse seems to say that every miracle Jesus performed can be done by us also—and even more. The real question is what *kind* of works did Jesus have in mind? Was he referring to physical works, the physical miracles?

One of the things we tend to forget is that Jesus did many physical miracles other than healing. He walked on the water, turned water into wine, fed five thousand men (not counting women and children) with a sack lunch, calmed a raging storm, and made a fish pay his income tax (now that's a miracle I would love to repeat). In summing up the earthly ministry of Jesus, the apostle John said, "Therefore many other signs Jesus also performed in the presence of the disciples, which are not written in this book" (John 20:30). He ends his account with these words: "And there are also many other things which Jesus did, which if they were written in detail, I suppose that even the world itself would not contain the books that would be written" (John 21:25).

During the period covered by the book of Acts, the apostles did work miracles of healing similar to those of Jesus, but we have no record that they duplicated his other "works," such as those mentioned above.

The works of Jesus include far more than acts of healing. Is it an honest handling of Scripture to select just one of these "works" and ignore the rest? If Jesus meant for us to replicate his physical miracles, then it follows that we ought to witness water turned into wine, the dead raised, multitudes fed with a handful of food, and fish caught with enough money in their mouths to pay our taxes.

Perhaps the real key to what Jesus meant is found in the phrase we often overlook: "because I go to the Father." Here Jesus makes it clear that the greater works of his followers is conditioned on his return to the Father. Why? Why was it necessary to ascend to the Father before the disciples could fulfill his promise? The ascension was certainly not essential to the working of physical miracles. They had been doing those for three years.

Upon ascending, Jesus would send the Holy Spirit (see John 7:39; 16:7) and occupy the place of intercession to hear and answer the prayers of his disciples. It was this that would make possible the doing of greater works.

Jesus is emphasizing the union that will exist between himself and his disciples, even though they will be separated physically. He is leaving them, but if they will continue to trust him, the work that he started will remain and even increase. His physical absence will make no difference—rather it will enhance their effectiveness. In other words, when they work, it will be Jesus working still; his works will be their works and their works his. Barnabas Lindars says, "As their works are the works of Jesus, they will be just as much the activity of God in the world as his own works were."[1]

"Works" and "greater works" refer not so much to the independent and specific acts of the disciples, but rather to the fact that everything they do will actually be Jesus doing it through them. The "greater works" of the disciples depend upon the "going" of Jesus. His ascent would mean the descent of the empowering Holy Spirit and the inauguration of Christ's heavenly intercession, thus enabling the church to fulfill its mission of evangelizing the world. For as J. C. Ryle pointed out, "'Greater works' mean more conversions. There is no greater work possible than the conversion of a soul."[2] (See rule 2 of biblical interpretation in chapter 9.)

Leon Morris writes,

> What Jesus means we may see in the narratives of the Acts. There are a few miracles of healing, but the emphasis is on the mighty work of conversion. On the day of Pentecost alone more believers were added to the little band of believers than throughout Christ's entire earthly life. There we see a literal fulfillment of "greater works than these shall be done." During His lifetime the Son of God was confined in His influence to a comparatively small sector of Palestine. After His departure His followers were able to work in widely scattered places and influence much larger numbers of men.[3]

Power to Heal, Power to Save?

Those who claim that the greater works are indeed the physical miracles of Jesus say that it takes the same power to save souls as it does to heal bodies. If we do not have the power to heal, then certainly we do not have the power to save. Healing power is proof of saving power. But they contradict their own argument by telling sick Christians they are not healed because they do not have enough faith. On the contrary, according to their interpretation of John 14:12, if sick Christians had the power to be saved, they should also have the power to be healed.

Further, they claim, if the world sees the power of God released in the healing of sick bodies, as well as other signs and wonders, the world will be convinced of the claims of Christ and believe. But this idea is based on the popular but erroneous notion that miracles produce faith. Psalm 78 vividly illustrates this. The psalm is a summary of all the wonderful miracles God performed for his people. If ever a people witnessed the unfettered power of God, the Israelites did. Yet the sad refrain repeats itself again and again: "They forgot His deeds and His miracles that He had shown them" (v. 11).

"In spite of all this they still sinned and did not believe in His wonderful works" (v. 32).

The single miracle of our Lord that each of the Gospels records is the miracle of the loaves, the feeding of the five thousand. John tells us that immediately the people attempted to make him king, by force if necessary (see John 6:15). But Jesus slipped away from the crowd. The next day the multitude sought him out. He responded by saying, "Truly, truly, I say to you, you seek Me, not because you saw signs, but because you ate of the loaves and were filled" (John 6:26).

Jesus then launched into a long, magnificent discourse on the Bread of Life. "Truly, truly, I say to you, unless you eat the flesh of the Son of Man and drink His blood, you have no life in yourselves" (John 6:53).

The conclusion of the whole episode is summed up by John in these words: "As a result of this many of His disciples withdrew and were not walking with Him anymore" (John 6:66). As long as Jesus satisfied their physical and material needs, they were willing to make him king. But when he stopped talking about bread and sardines and insisted on something infinitely higher—personal commitment to himself—most everyone but the Twelve lost interest and took off. Faith created by bread will always "turn back" when the bread runs out. These fickle followers were motivated by physical desires and material needs. It has always been that way. The multitude has always cried, "Feed us and we will make you king!" Dostoevsky's *The Grand Inquisitor* describes the Devil's temptation of Christ to turn stones into bread in these words: "Do you see those stones in this parched and barren desert? Turn them into loaves of bread and men will follow You like cattle, grateful and docile, although constantly fearful lest You withdraw Your hand and they lose Your loaves."

Jesus never made miracles the foundation of faith. (See discussion under "Why Then the Miracles?" in chapter 12.) The miracles were intended to authenticate his claim to be the messiah; they were never meant to be the means of converting the lost to faith in Christ. We follow him for his sake, not for the sake of our stomach or our personal comfort.

We are too easily impressed with miracles. We fawn over them. To us they are the credentials of real faith and of the true work of God. Everything must be extraordinary; the commonplace is unacceptable. Jesus found it so in his day. But even when his enemies saw the miracles, they discounted them by asking, "Is this not the carpenter's son? Is not His mother called Mary, and His brothers, James and Joseph and Simon and Judas? And His sisters, are they not all with us? Where then did this man get all these things? And they took offense at Him" (Matt. 13:55–57). In their opinion, Jesus was too ordinary to be extraordinary, too common to be uncommon.

As a means of producing faith, miracles are highly suspect. Miracles do not produce faith, and faith that claims its origin in a miracle is questionable. The rich man in hell (see Luke 16:19–31) reasoned that a visitor from the grave would persuade his brothers to turn to God. Sounds like a good idea to me. Surely something as spectacular as that would persuade them. But listen to the answer: "If they do not listen to Moses and the Prophets, they will not be persuaded even if someone rises from the dead" (Luke 16:31).

John MacArthur writes,

> We must realize that even if Christians would
> heal everybody the way Jesus did, everyone would
> not believe the Gospel. After all Jesus' marvelous
> healings, what did the people do? They crucified
> him. The same was true for the apostles. They did
> miracle after miracle of healing. And what hap-
> pened? They were jailed, persecuted, even killed.
> Salvation never comes through getting healed. It
> is a gift from God according to his sovereign will.
> Salvation is given to whom God wills, and it comes
> through hearing and believing the Gospel. As Paul
> wrote, "Faith comes by hearing, and hearing by the
> word of Christ." (Rom. 10:17)[4]

It is true that, according to John 14:12, Christ has given the
church power to equal and exceed his works. But these greater
works are spiritual victories, not physical miracles. From the
viewpoint of the New Testament, the spiritual is always to be
desired above the physical. It is greater to save from sin than to
heal from sickness. Faith in God and faith in miracles are not
synonymous.

The Unchanging Christ of Hebrews 13:8

Teachers of "signs and wonders" often quote Hebrews 13:8:
"Jesus Christ is the same yesterday and today and forever." They
assert that what happened during the earthly ministry of Jesus
and the apostolic age is normative for Christianity because Jesus
has not changed. He is the same today as he was yesterday. Since
Christ healed the sick while on earth, shouldn't we expect him

to do the same today, since he is the same "yesterday and today and forever"? And since the apostles performed numerous healings and other miracles after Pentecost, can we not see the same miracles today, being in the same Pentecostal dispensation?

But Hebrews 13:8 is not a proof text for healing. (See how rule 5 in chapter 10 applies here.) Verse 8 links verses 7 and 9. In verse 7, the writer speaks of former leaders who are gone; their memory lives on, but they can no longer guide us. But Jesus Christ is always available to us for counsel and guidance. Human leaders upon whom we lean for counsel may be carried by death beyond our reach. But Jesus remains the same through every generation.

Then in verse 9 the writer warns his readers not to be carried away by all kinds of strange teaching, for Jesus is God's last and unchanging message to humankind. Since he is sufficiently the same, no other teaching can supersede or supplant him.

The central thought is *Christ is unchanging in his character*. Because of this, we are to be unchanging in our faith. Jesus Christ is the same today as he was yesterday—in his character, in his nature, in his attributes. In his essential essence Jesus remains unchanged.

But he is not the same in his manifestation and activity. He never has been. Jesus did not begin at Bethlehem. To write his biography you must go far behind the manger to find his beginnings. Even standing on the dark edge of eternity past and peering into the blackness of that unknown region, you will not be able to trace his origin. He has no beginning just as he has no end; he is the eternal Now.

Until Bethlehem no one knew God had a Son. But whether wrapped in swaddling clothes and lying in a manger, mystifying the scholars in the temple, teaching thousands on the shores of Galilee, or hanging between two thieves on a Roman gibbet, he was the same. But the same only in the essentials—grace, love, mercy, and all the other qualities possessed by the God of grace. And while these virtues have always been manifested, they have never worn the same garments in every dispensation. No one would insist that Jesus was the same in his manifestation in the Old Testament as he was in the New.

It is worth noting that we have no record of Jesus healing anyone after his resurrection. In his introduction to the book of Acts, Luke tells us that Jesus "presented Himself alive after His suffering by many convincing proofs, appearing to them over a period of forty days and speaking of the things concerning the kingdom of God" (Acts 1:3).

By many convincing proofs for forty days Jesus showed himself to be alive. Yet no miracle of healing is mentioned among the convincing proofs. For Jesus personally, the time of healing was past; his messiahship had been authenticated by his resurrection. His disciples would perform miracles to authenticate their message that Jesus had truly risen from the grave. But for Jesus, healings were no longer needed, no longer an essential part of his ministry.

Have you ever wondered why there is a conspicuous absence of references to the earthly miracles of Jesus in the Epistles of the New Testament? Not one of the writers ever refers back to the miracles performed during his earthly sojourn. No one mentions that he healed anyone. He is not called "Christ the Healer," and there is no indication that the miracles of healing should continue today as they did then.

Are Signs and Wonders Needed Today?

The apostle John settles this issue by his statement in John 20:30–31: "Many other signs Jesus also performed in the presence of the disciples, which are not written in this book; but these have been written so that you may believe that Jesus is the Christ, the Son of God; and that believing you may have life in His name." John records seven "signs":

1. Turning water into wine at Cana (2:1–11);
2. Healing the nobleman's son (4:46–54);
3. Healing the paralytic (5:1–15);
4. Feeding the five thousand (6:1–14);
5. Walking on the water (6:16–21);
6. Healing the blind man (9:1–7);
7. Raising Lazarus from the dead (11:1–44).

These signs, says John, are sufficient for me to believe on the name of Jesus and be saved. To insist that new signs and wonders are needed today for the conversion of unbelievers is to say that the Word of God, the Bible as we have it, is defective and ineffectual. The only signs necessary to bring about saving faith in Christ are the ones recorded in John's Gospel. And if people will not believe those, they will not be persuaded even though one rose from the dead.

The next point we must address builds on this one: Has God given the present-day church the same miraculous healing ministry he gave to Jesus and the apostles? If he has, there should be an unmistakable similarity between healings in the New Testament and those of our time. We'll examine this point in the next chapter.

CHAPTER 12

The Healings of Jesus and the Apostles: A Closer Look

Are They Valid Models for Modern-Day Healing?

ONE OF JESUS' ACTIVITIES AS he moved about the countryside was healing the sick and those beset by evil spirits. If that's true, why should we not see similar manifestations today? I agree that miracles of healing played an important role in our Lord's earthly ministry. The various Greek words used to express the idea of healing appear more than eighty times in the New Testament, seventy-five of which are found in the Synoptic Gospels (Matthew, Mark, and Luke) and in Acts. Howard Clark Kee writes,

> Of the approximately 250 literary units into which the first three gospels are divided, one fifth either describe or allude to the healing and exorcistic activities of Jesus and the disciples. Of the seven "signs" reported in John to have been done

by Jesus, four involve healing or restoration. Of the seventy literary units in John, twelve either describe his healing activity or refer to the signs which he performed.[1]

The first mention of healing serves as an important part of the introduction to the public ministry of Jesus. "Jesus was going throughout all Galilee, teaching in their synagogues and proclaiming the gospel of the kingdom, and healing every kind of disease and every kind of sickness among the people. The news about Him spread throughout all Syria; and they brought to Him all who were ill, those suffering with various diseases and pains, demoniacs, epileptics, paralytics; and He healed them" (Matt. 4:23–24).

Healing: Then and Now

As I mentioned earlier, the issue we're dealing with is not only whether God heals today, but whether the earthly ministry of Jesus and the apostles has been restored to modern Christianity. Has God given to the present-day church the same miraculous ministry he gave to Jesus and the apostles? If he has, there will be an unmistakable similarity between the New Testament and the healings of today. In this chapter we will examine the characteristics of New Testament healing to see if they compare to the healing of today.

The Diseases and Disabilities Cured by Jesus and the Apostles Were at That Time Considered Incurable; the Majority Remain So Today

Broadly speaking, physical disorders fall into two categories: organic and functional. Organic diseases are those in which some change in the structure of the body tissue can be identified. These changes may be seen by the eye or under a microscope, they may be seen by a routine X-ray or a scan, or they may be detected by a blood or urine specimen or biopsy. Ultimately, organic disease can be proven by an abnormality in the body tissue that can be seen by the eye, a microscope X-ray, or a laboratory study. Cancer, pneumonia, meningitis, polio, rheumatoid arthritis, and diabetes are examples of organic diseases

In contrast, functional disorders are much harder to evaluate because there is seldom any kind of structural defect. In other words, no change in the structure of the body tissue can be detected. This is not to say that the symptoms are imagined or the pain supposed. They are real, but they are caused by a change in the *function* of the tissue, not in structure.

Chronic stress, anxiety, fatigue, and bad eating habits can cause an organ to function abnormally, resulting in real physical symptoms such as headaches, back spasms, chest pain, and dizziness. There is nothing structurally wrong with the organ itself, but it is behaving as if there were.

Physicians tell us that many functional disorders are associated with certain types of personality. Others may be determined by the genetics of a person and triggered by an emotional trauma such as stress, tension, anger, or anxiety. The "businessman's special," the peptic ulcer, is a psychosomatic disease provoked by emotional disturbances like stress, worry, or even fatigue. And where there is a predisposition to it, asthma is a functional disturbance, a way of expressing inner anguish. In short, chronic stress can produce a functional change in the organs.

When a person is emotionally or spiritually out of balance, his body begins to function abnormally. Physicians describe this as "psychophysiologic"—functional abnormalities resulting from stresses to the psyche. And this eventually leads to psychosomatic disorder. Regarding psychophysiologic and psychosomatic disorders, Dr. Paul Tournier says, "The terror of past centuries was the scourge of great epidemics such as cholera, plague, and puerperal fever . . . in this field . . . the success of medicine is a veritable triumph. Unhappily, a specter menaces humanity today—its nervous state."[2] He goes on to say that the number of psychopathic conditions, functional disorders, neuroses, and psychoses have increased catastrophically over the last few years.

Doctors agree that the vast majority of disorders they treat start out as functional disorders brought on by stress, tension, or emotional or physical exhaustion. If you ask your doctor, "Am I really sick, or is it all in my head?" he will probably say something like, "We prefer not to separate the mind from the body."

Trained in the day when the study of medicine is dominated by pathologic anatomy (organic illness), it is easy to understand the frustration doctors and their patients feel when they are unable to pronounce a precise diagnosis and name an exact category into which the problem may be placed.

Symptoms such as dizziness, nausea, headaches, and backaches may represent an organic illness, or they may simply be the result of a functional disorder related to stress fatigue. In and of itself, stress can cause functional abnormalities of many organs resulting in various symptoms that would go away if the stress were relieved. Consequently, it is no mystery when "faith healing" sometimes works.

Jesus healed organic disorders such as crippled legs, withered hands, blind eyes, deaf ears—cases in which there was no question a miracle had occurred. The healings accomplished by Jesus and his disciples were not, as many are today, natural remissions, psychosomatic cures, or minor functional disorders that would have corrected themselves, like the seven-day cold or the twenty-four-hour virus.

Jesus Healed with a Word or a Touch

The only record we have of Jesus using a secondary means is John 9:6. "When He had said this, He spat on the ground, and made clay of the spittle, and applied the clay to his eyes." No explanation is given as to why Jesus used clay in this instance. Perhaps he was making it clear that he was not bound by one method. No mention is made that Jesus ever employed the most common oriental aid, anointing oil.

Jesus Healed Everyone Who Came for Healing

The Lord was remarkably successful in his healing ministry. Unlike modern healers, no disappointed people returned from his meeting still bound to wheelchairs or crutches. There were no failures. There were no unhealed people to accuse of unbelief or unconfessed sin.

And he did it smoothly and quietly. Watching some healers perform, I have feared for the safety of the person whose head was jerked back and forth, accompanied by frenzied shouts and pounding. With Jesus there was no long, drawn-out, loud praying, pleading, and pounding. He just did it. And no one ever went away disappointed or embarrassed. Jesus never had to face puzzled believers and explain his failure.

Jesus Healed without Regard to Faith, as Well as with It

This is surprising when we consider the great emphasis placed on faith as being indispensable to healing. While many of the healings of Jesus were in response to faith, he never made faith a necessary requirement. Some of his most notable miracles were performed without any reference to faith whatsoever.

No mention of faith is made in the healing of Peter's mother-in-law (see Matt. 8:14–15). The same is true of the leper in Matthew 8:1–4 and of the man with the withered hand in Matthew 12:10–13. In some cases those who were healed had no idea they were going to be made whole.

But what about Matthew 13:58: "And He did not do many miracles there because of their unbelief"? When Jesus went to his hometown, Nazareth, to teach in the synagogue, the people were astonished. This was nothing more than a carpenter's son, they clamored. He was a hometown boy; they had seen him grow up, had played together in the dusty streets of Nazareth. No, this man is not the One we should look for. Matthew's account closes with these words: "And He did not do many miracles there because of their unbelief." But the reference wasn't to their unbelief in Jesus as a healer. It was their unbelief in Jesus as the promised Messiah.

Mary and Martha believed that Jesus could have healed their brother while he was still alive, but they had trouble believing that he could raise Lazarus from the grave. I doubt that Malchus, the soldier whose ear Peter sliced off in the garden, was a believer in Jesus or had any faith that his ear could be restored. And the Gerasene maniac of Mark 5 certainly was not exercising faith when Jesus made him whole. Peter and John healed a lame man who was expecting, not a miracle, but a coin (see Acts 3:1–11).

Claus Westermann, discussing Abraham's reaction to the news that a son from Sarah (not Hagar's son, Ishmael) would be the son of promise (see Gen. 17:18), says that Abraham's prayer for Ishmael "implies that he does not believe the promise of a son to Sarah." He goes on to say that "God fulfills his promise without being bound to Abraham's faith; what God has promised he does, independently of human attitudes."[3]

And then Jesus healed some, not because of *their* faith, but in response to the faith of others. Take the case of the centurion's servant: After listening to his pleas on behalf of the servant, Jesus said to the centurion, "Go; it shall be done for you as you have believed" (Matt. 8:13).

Also there is the familiar incident of the crippled man whose four friends lowered him through a roof to get to Jesus. "Seeing *their* faith, He said, 'Friend, your sins are forgiven you'" (Luke 5:20). John tells the story of the nobleman's son who was healed because of his father's faith (see John 4:50).

Further on we will look more closely at the healing passage in the fifth chapter of James, but for now let's observe one thing. The passage reads, "Is anyone among you sick? Then he must call for the *elders* of the church and *they are to pray* over him, anointing him with oil in the name of the Lord; and *the prayer offered in faith* will restore the one who is sick" (James 5:14–15). Notice that it is the elders of the church who are to pray over the afflicted, and it is their prayer of faith, not that of the afflicted, that secures the healing.

But I have never heard a faith healer admit that it was his own lack of faith that hindered the healing of a sick person. Blame is always placed at the feet of the unhealed. The "lack of faith" excuse is a handy escape clause for would-be-healers. It allows them to walk away from their failures, from the smashed hopes, the frustrated faith, the guilt-laden hearts, the embarrassing deaths, free of all responsibility and absolved of all the blame.

Jesus Healed Instantaneously, Immediately, and Completely

"And Jesus said to the centurion, 'Go; it shall be done for you as you have believed.' And the servant was healed that very moment" (Matt 8:13).

"Immediately the flow of her blood was dried up; and she felt in her body that she was healed of her affliction" (Mark 5:29).

"When He saw them, He said to them, 'Go and show yourselves to the priests.' And as they were going, they were cleansed"

(Luke 17:14). The phrase "as they were going" does not indicate a gradual healing; the word *cleansed* is a Greek aorist tense, which here signals an all-at-once happening.

In Luke 6:10, we find another account of immediate healing— this time a withered hand. "After looking around at them all, he said to him, 'Stretch out your hand!' And he did so; and his hand was restored."

The healing of the lame man at Bethesda is recorded by John: "Jesus said to him, 'Get up, pick up your pallet and walk,' Immediately the man became well, and picked up his pallet and began to walk" (John 5:8–9).

Another significant point about the New Testament healings: They were abrupt, sudden, almost unexpected. Jesus did not require several days of preparation in which time the afflicted person was to confess every sin, get thoroughly right with God and his neighbor, fast three days, and so forth.

And there was never follow-up advice about keeping a positive mental attitude and holding fast the confession of faith. The nearest thing to that is when Jesus warned the lame man healed at Bethesda, "Behold, you have become well; do not sin anymore, so that nothing worse happens to you" (John 5:14). But the man was healed instantly.

One writer offers this counsel:

> Turn a promise of healing into an affirmation and keep declaring it until you are fully convinced of its reality, until you believe it in your heart without wavering; and you will see that your symptoms disappear. . . . Repeat such affirmations aloud many times a day. Spend five or ten or fifteen minutes a day affirming aloud these declarations, and you will find that they are true and that His resurrection

life will be manifested in your mortal body. Your
symptoms will pass away. They will vanish in direct
proportion to the clarity and strength of your faith.
The moment your faith is perfect, that moment you
will be completely delivered.[4]

This is representative of the follow-up counsel often given to
those who claim healing. But this kind of advice has no parallel
in Scripture. Not one of the healing miracles recorded in the New
Testament came about in the manner described—and never were
the healed advised to do the things the writer suggests.

To say that our faith must become perfect before we are
completely delivered ignores the fact that, with only a couple of
exceptions, everyone who came to Jesus for a miracle came with
a weak and imperfect faith. Yet Jesus responded to the faith they
had, because in faith the supreme matter is not its size, but its
object, which is Jesus.

PMA (Positive Mental Attitude) routines are often justified
by quoting Hebrews 10:23: "Let us hold fast the confession of
our hope without wavering, for He who promised is faithful."
But using this verse to shore up the walls of atonement healing
violates its contextual integrity. This verse has nothing to do with
healing, as the context clearly shows. It deals with apostasy and
faith in Jesus as the promised Messiah and High Priest, not as
Healer.

"But" you say, "it worked for me!" I believe you. The method
is effective for certain functional ailments. But again, the issue
is not whether it works but whether it is what the Bible says. Are
we seeing the healing miracles of Jesus duplicated today? In other
words, is it being done now the same way he did it then? The clear
answer is no.

Sickness or Symptoms?

The healings of Jesus were immediate and complete. You will not find people in the Bible healed but continuing to suffer the symptoms of their illness. Statements such as "You are healed; your body just doesn't know it yet" and "Believe God, not your symptoms" have no biblical foundation and are foreign to any miracles Jesus or his apostles performed. What value is there in being healed of a cold if you continue to cough and sneeze and run fever for the next seven days? Much worse, it presents a mighty weak witness to the world to insist that God has healed me while it is obvious to everyone else I am still suffering. What kind of God is it who has power to take away the sickness but not the suffering it causes?

And What Kind of Father Is God?

A friend was dying of cancer. He and many others had claimed his healing as his divine right in Christ. But he died. A mutual friend tried to juggle atonement healing in one hand and our friend's death in the other by explaining, "He had faith—but evidently it weakened at the end and he forfeited his healing."

What kind of God is this? What kind of father would treat his child with such calculating coldness? Can you imagine a father saying to his drowning child, "I'll save you if you have perfect faith. But if your faith falters, even after your hand is in mine, I'll let you go, and you'll slip beneath the water." Thus faith becomes a human achievement, and holds no hope for those who are weak and need help the most. This is not the Father Jesus came to reveal.

There Were No Recorded Relapses

Neither in the Gospels nor in the Acts is there any indication that someone healed by Jesus or his disciples ever suffered a relapse. Yet it cannot be denied that in today's healing movement countless cases of relapse occur. Wade Boggs observes that "the multitudes who hear . . . public testimonies to healing rarely learn the sequels to the alleged cures. There are cases where persons pronounced incurably ill by doctors mistakenly believe themselves cured . . . only to suffer relapse later."[5]

The truth is, no layperson is qualified either to diagnose his own disease or pronounce his own recovery. Even fully qualified doctors often disagree regarding the diagnosis of a single patient, and sometimes all of them are wrong. "Public testimonies of healings at moments of great excitement and emotional stress are worthless."[6]

Jesus Raised the Dead

Jesus wasn't afraid to hold a meeting in a graveyard or put his reputation on the line by designating which corpse (Lazarus) should rise. But modern healers give funeral parlors and cemeteries a wide berth.

In recent years many books and magazine articles have appeared chronicling the experiences of people who died and lived to tell about it. Most of them "died" on the operating table. Some went to heaven; others hovered over their own body, watching the surgeons fighting to resuscitate them. And the doctors were successful. But a person heavily sedated for surgery is not a reliable witness. Experience cannot authenticate itself.

Suffice it to say that those who have experienced "clinical" death were, as Hans Kung puts it, dying but not dead. They were almost dead but didn't quite make it.[7]

Every once in a while reports filter in of someone being raised from the dead, someone who was *really* dead and buried. But if a really dead person (I mean someone like Lazarus—dead, embalmed, and buried four days) was raised from the dead, you wouldn't have to hear about it through some obscure grapevine. It would be splattered across the front page of every newspaper in the country. Ted Koppel would have him on camera before he could get out of his grave-clothes.

Speaking of the successful healings of Jesus and his apostles, J. I. Packer writes, "Whatever else can be said of the ministry of the Pentecostal and charismatic healers of our time and of those whose praying for the sick has become a matter, as it seems, of specific divine calling, none of them has a track record like this."[8]

As a Rule, Jesus Discouraged, Often Forbade, the Publicizing of His Healing Miracles

As I studied the characteristics of the biblical healings, I was not surprised by most of what I found, namely the points I just shared. But this one caught me off guard. I had never considered such a thing because it is in such sharp contrast to modern practices. When we witness the healing of a person, especially one declared incurable by reputable doctors, we are overwhelmed with excitement and we want to get the word out. And this is as it should be, or so it seems. But Jesus shunned such publicity.

To the leper, Jesus said, "See that you tell no one" (Matt. 8:4).

To the two blind men, "Jesus sternly warned them: 'See that no one knows about this!" (Matt 9:30).

After healing a multitude, Jesus "warned them not to tell who He was" (Matt. 12:16).

When he healed the deaf man with the speech impediment, "He gave them orders not to tell anyone" (Mark 7:36).

After raising the daughter of Jairus, Jesus instructed the parents "to tell no one what had happened" (Luke 8:56).

The Danger of Overshadowing His Mission

Jesus knew people would be overly excited by the news of such miracles and assume, incorrectly, that he was about to set up a splendid earthly kingdom. For instance, when Jesus fed the multitude, the people said, "'This is truly the Prophet who is to come into the world.' So Jesus, perceiving that they were intending to come and take Him by force to make Him king, withdrew again to the mountain by Himself alone" (John 6:14–15).

In Mark 1:45, we read that the cleansed leper, ignoring the warning of Jesus, "went out and began to proclaim it freely and to spread the news around, *to such an extent that Jesus could no longer publicly enter a city*, but stayed out in unpopulated areas and they were coming to Him from everywhere."

The exception in Mark 5:19 proves the rule. There Jesus tells a man to publicize what had been done for him because it was in a region where there was no danger of a popular uprising to make him a king. On the contrary, there was a very unfavorable sentiment toward him, which Jesus wanted to correct.

Later Jesus made several distant trips for the purpose of escaping the people and preventing the wrong kind of excitement about him.

Plainly, Jesus did not want the miracles to overshadow the real purpose of his coming. With such elation over the healings the real issue would become clouded. He knew men, knew that they were more interested in miracles than in the faith that produced them. They followed him for the bread.

But this, of course, was in keeping with prophecy. In Matthew 12:15–21, we read,

> But Jesus . . . warned them not to tell who He was.
>> This was to fulfill what was spoken through
>> Isaiah the prophet:
> "Behold, my servant whom I have chosen'
> My beloved in whom my soul is well-pleased;
> I will put my spirit upon him,
> And he shall proclaim justice to the gentiles.
> He will not quarrel, nor cry out;
> Nor will anyone hear his voice in the streets.
> A battered reed he will not break off,
> And a smoldering wick he will not put out,
> Until he leads justice to victory.
> And in his name the gentiles will hope."

Times haven't changed that much; human nature hasn't changed at all. Let's face it—we're human. We get more excited over the physical healing of a sick person than the salvation of a lost person.

Suppose next Sunday morning two things happen in your worship service: A man, crippled from birth, is suddenly and miraculously healed; at the same time a young boy trusts Christ as his Savior and Lord. Which of these two happenings ignite the people's interest? Which one will they go away shouting about? Without a doubt, the physical healing. But compare the two: One is a physical miracle, the other a spiritual one. One is temporal, for the man will eventually die; the other is eternal because the boy is saved forever. The physical miracle requires only a word from God; the spiritual miracle, the salvation of the boy, costs God his only Son.

It's no mystery why the health-and-wealth movement is so popular. It thrives because it appeals to the sensual. Recently a local citizen was asked why he voted for a certain political candidate. He answered candidly, "He gives us what we want."

Vance Havner confirms this tendency of human nature: "Today when converts from awful lives of sin tell their story—and thank God for every one of them—the congregation 'oohs' and 'ahs'; but let a man tell simply of being kept from childhood by the grace of God and their reaction is often 'so what?' A story of being healed of cancer is top news but to tell of good health to old age by the same God who heals the sick is poor show biz."[9]

Sincere preachers may intend healing to be simply a means of pointing people to Christ, but the "healings" have a way of seizing the spotlight and upstaging salvation. The spotlight that should focus on Jesus is shifted to the physical miracles, and they become Exhibit A in the case for faith. They become the catalyst for praise and worship.

Promoting physical healing, making it the heart of our advertising and the strength of our attraction, violated both the command and the example of our Lord. This one fact alone makes it clear that the modern health-and-wealth movement is biblically unsound and unsafe.

Why Then the Miracles?

The miracles of Christ belonged to the day in which they were performed. They were the supernatural credentials of Jesus' messiahship. They were signs for then, not guarantees for now, not models for modern preachers.

John the Baptist, after being cast into prison by Herod, was besieged by doubts concerning the identity of Christ and sent word, asking, "Are You the Expected One, or shall we look for someone else?" (Matt. 11:3). Jesus did not rebuke him for doubting but sent word back to him: "Go and report to John what you hear and see: the blind receive sight and the lame walk, the lepers are cleansed and the deaf hear, the dead are raised up, and the poor have the gospel preached to them" (Matt. 11:4–5).

As the apostle John drew his gospel to a close, he said, "Many other signs Jesus also performed in the presence of the disciples, which are not written in this book; but these have been written so that you may believe that Jesus is the Christ, the son of God; and that believing you may have life in His name" (John 20:30–31).

The miracles were not ends in themselves; they were means to an end, a greater end. I am not saying that Jesus cared nothing for the physical suffering of those around him or that his healings were not motivated by compassion. But one act can serve two purposes. John, with the other Gospel writers, shows that the primary purpose of the physical miracles of Jesus was not to heal, but to present irrefutable evidence of his messiahship.

And the same is true of the miracles performed by the apostles—they were meant to authenticate the apostolic message and ministry.

Today, with the Bible complete and the witness of the indwelling presence and power of the Spirit, the need for authentication by Christ's miracles has passed.

A Closing Word

God often does extraordinary things during extraordinary times, such as times of revival and spiritual awakening. Within that context there are unusual manifestations of his power, but they are meant to arrest the attention of the multitudes and attest to the authenticity of the message. The demand that such unusual and extraordinary happenings be the norm of the everyday life of the church is a misunderstanding and misinterpretation of God's ways and works.

Again I quote J. Sidlow Baxter:

> Neither from our Lord's miracles nor from those of the Apostles can we safely deduce that such are meant to continue today, nor should we presume so. If such healing were divinely intended to continue in the same way today, then all who came for healing today would be healed without exception, as was the case in the days of our Lord and the Apostles. But thousands who come for healing are not healed. Therefore by that simple, practical test we know that healings today are not on the same basis as in those days of long ago.[10]

Neither Baxter nor I are saying that God does not heal today. God does. I am simply suggesting that, based on the criteria developed in this chapter, the healings of the New Testament are not intended to be models for healings today. God has a far different purpose in mind for us. In some cases, healing may be his design for accomplishing that purpose—in other situations, he may choose to wait or to say no in order to bring about his purpose. The question for us becomes "Do I want my pleasure or his purpose? On which should I focus my heart?"

CHAPTER 13

Did Christ Die to Make Us Healthy?

Do You Have the Right to Be Healed?

DO THE FOLLOWING SCENARIOS SOUND familiar?

When a friend entered the hospital for surgery, the outcome of which was uncertain and might be the prelude to a long and terminal illness, a fellow church member unhesitatingly announced to him, "Remember, you have the right to be healed."

During a period of debilitating physical problems, which were more of a nuisance than a danger, I was told, "You know you don't have to put up with that. God wants you well."

These two statements, "You have a right to be healed" and "God wants you well," form the *crux interpretum*, the major point of the issue. Do we have the *right* to be healed? Does God want us well? Must we put up with sickness and suffering? Was it necessary for Paul to arrive at Galatia ill (see Gal. 4:13–15)? Did the apostle have to tolerate the thorn in his flesh (see 2 Cor. 12:7–10)? Was Epaphroditus sick unnecessarily (see Phil. 2:25–30)? Why didn't Paul suggest healing instead of wine for Timothy's stomach (see 1 Tim. 5:23)? Was it necessary that Paul leave Trophimus sick at Miletus (see 2 Tim. 4:20).

Is healing in the atonement, or is that a position not in keeping with what the Bible teaches, according to the rules of interpretation we've examined? When we use the word *atonement*, we mean the covering of sin, accomplished by the death of Christ on the cross. Leon Morris says, "Put simply, the atonement means that Jesus Christ in His death dealt completely with the problem that man's sin had set. Whatever had to be done, He did it, and now those who come in faith may enter into full salvation."[1] But did his blood also cover our sickness? Many believe that it did, that healing is in the atonement.

Atonement healing, the idea that both physical healing for the body and forgiveness for sins was obtained by Christ's death, runs something like this: (1) Sickness is the result of the fall; therefore, all sickness is the result of sin. Specific sicknesses may be caused by specific sins. (2) Christ's death on the cross made atonement for sin and its consequences, restoring to humankind all he forfeited in the fall. Thus Christ's death not only delivers people from sin, but also from the consequences of sin, sickness. (3) It is the right of every believer, therefore, to claim healing from any and all physical maladies. In other words, Christ's death saves us from sickness as well as from sin. Healing of the body is just as much a part of the gospel as is forgiveness of sins. This is often referred to as "the full gospel."

But is this what the Bible teaches about the atonement? When the first high priest, Aaron, entered the holy place with a bull offering, it was an offering for sin, not sickness (see Lev. 16:3). In verses 5–6, 11, 16, 21, and 34 of the same chapter it is obvious that all the sacrifices made were meant to atone for the sin of the people, not their sickness.

When the author of Hebrews spoke of Christ as the High Priest of the new covenant, he said, "But when Christ appeared as a high priest of the good things to come, He entered through the greater and more perfect tabernacle, not made with hands, that is to say, not of this creation; and not through the blood of goats and calves, but through His own blood, He entered the holy place once for all, having obtained eternal redemption" (Heb. 9:11–12). Both the Levitical record and the Hebrews letter make it plain that God was dealing with sin, not sickness.

Insisting that Christ atoned for our sickness betrays a lack of understanding, both of the atonement and of sickness. Christ died for our sin, not our sickness. Sickness is not a sin, thus it needs no atonement; it is one of the many results of sin. There were other consequences of the fall besides sickness—man must earn his living by the sweat of his brow, woman must struggle and suffer pain in childbirth, just to mention a couple. And yet I have never heard anyone claim atonement for these things, and as far as I can tell they are still very much with us. Even when the Old Testament speaks of God healing diseases, it never says God *forgives* disease; disease needs neither forgiveness nor atonement, for it is not a sin.

As long as men sweat, women agonize in pain during childbirth, snakes slither on their stomachs, and the thorns on a rosebush prick my finger, I must believe that the results of the fall have not been removed.

The heart of the argument for atonement healing lies in two passages in the New Testament. The first is Matthew 8:16–17: "When evening came, they brought to Him many who were demon-possessed; and he cast out the spirits with a word, and healed all who were ill. This was to fulfill what was spoken through Isaiah the prophet: 'He Himself took our infirmities and carried away our diseases.'"

When was this statement made? These words were spoken nearly three years before the cross, and yet Matthew claims the prophecy of Isaiah was fulfilled then and there, at the specific moment.

In the Gospel accounts of the crucifixion many prophecies are said to have been realized, but never this one. It is reasonable to assume that if Isaiah's prophecy meant Christ would atone for sickness, it would be found with the crucifixion accounts. But it is not. If the words in Matthew 8:16–17 had been recorded at the crucifixion, they would be compelling evidence for atonement healing (see rule 5 in chapter 10). The truth is the prophecy of Matthew refers to the earthly public ministry of Christ, as verse 16 makes clear.

Further, the Greek word used for "carried" or "bore," *bastadzo,* is *never* used in the New Testament in connection with Christ's bearing our sin. The word is used in the New Testament to express the idea of sympathetic bearing, such as in Galatians 6:2 and Romans 15:1.

Not only that, but in 2 Corinthians 12:9 (KJV) Paul declares that he glories in this "infirmities." *Infirmities* translates the same Greek word used in Matthew 8:17: "our infirmities." How could Paul glory in something that Christ took away when he died?

The second New Testament text is found in 1 Peter 2:24. This verse is a quotation from Isaiah 53: "And He Himself bore our sins in His body on the cross, so that we might die to sin and live to righteousness; for by His wounds you were healed." There is little to comment on here because an honest reading of the text shows that Peter was speaking of spiritual healing from sin, not physical healing from sickness. Here again the Bible is concerned with sin.

But conceding for a moment that healing is in the atonement, the same could be said for the elimination of death, the banishment of all sorrow, the end of pain. Death as a consequence of the fall is emphasized in the Bible much more than sickness; if the atonement removed all the results of the fall, why do Christians still die?

We do not possess everything the atonement purchased for us. There is salvation to come, the redemption of the body. Peter writes of being "protected by the power of God through faith for a salvation ready to be revealed in the last time" (1 Pet. 1:5). And with Paul, we are "waiting eagerly for our adoption as sons, the redemption of our body" (Rom. 8:23). Meanwhile, with the rest of creation, we groan within ourselves. Margaret Clarkson, no stranger to suffering, writes,

> Physical suffering, along with evils of every kind, is ours because of man's sin. . . . Christians have no right to isolate illness and seek to exorcise it from our lives as if it were the ultimate evil. We are meant to war on all the wretched consequences of sin, not just one of them. To focus our efforts unduly on sickness is to ignore other evils equally if not more important.[2]

Healing versus Forgiveness

If healing is as much a part of the atonement as forgiveness of sin, we should be able to receive it as simply as we receive forgiveness. But we know that is not so. God has promised to save all who come to him for salvation; he has not promised to heal all those who come to him for healing.

Forgiveness covers all sin and every kind of sin. The same cannot be said of healing. Missing teeth are not replaced, amputated limbs are not restored, many faith healers wear glasses, and some wear toupees.

Forgiveness is immediate, but even the advocates of atonement healing admit that healing is often gradual and in stages.

Forgiveness of sin is never withheld because the sinner hasn't enough faith. I have been a minister more than forty years, and I have yet to see God refuse salvation to anyone who called on his name. But when healing doesn't come, people claim insufficient faith as the reason. If healing is on a par with forgiveness, why isn't it as easily obtained? How much faith is enough?

I have enough faith to be saved; why don't I have enough faith to be healed? Surely salvation of the soul is more precious than healing of the body—why is God so liberal with forgiveness and so stingy with healing.

Christ did not commission us to preach healing of the body and forgiveness of sins. "And He said to them, 'Thus it is written, that the Christ would suffer and rise again from the dead the third day, and the repentance for forgiveness of sins would be proclaimed in His name to all the nations, beginning from Jerusalem'" (Luke 24:46–47). Again, I quote Wade Boggs:

> When Paul outlined the essential content of
> the Gospel in 1 Corinthians 15:1–3, he made no
> mention of a right to physical healing based on the
> atonement as part of the Gospel message. . . . In the
> preaching and writings of Peter and John there is
> no word of a Gospel of healing for all, rooted in the
> atonement. Is it really conceivable that the Apostles
> and the authors of the New Testament were them-
> selves preaching only a half-gospel? I think not.[3]

Atonement healing is inconsistent with both experience and Scripture; there is no solid biblical basis for the doctrine. The gospel of physical healing is an errant gospel, and it offers false hope to those who listen. Leslie Weatherhead wrote, "It is no wonder that healing missions produce in many people black depression and hopeless despair. Most of those who attend are not healed, and their last estate is often worse than the first."[4]

Atonement healing doesn't square with the facts. It just isn't so. It doesn't work. I wish it did. But Christians of every spiritual echelon still get sick, stay sick, and die. After all the explanations put forth by teachers of this doctrine, one question always remains unanswered—it will not go away: "why are some healed while others are not?"

C. R. Brown, in his classic book *Faith and Health*, observes, "No public testimony meetings are ever held where the people who have tried to be cured by faith and have failed are invited to speak. If they were, these suffers . . . would outnumber the others a hundred to one."[5]

If God did not provide healing in the atonement, could he still be committed to our health and wellness as believers? Or is the promise of health another misunderstanding of Scripture? We'll examine the issue in the next chapter.

CHAPTER 14

Does God Always Want Us Well?

The Harmful Side Effects of Unscriptural Teaching

SOME WHO PROMOTE ATONEMENT HEALING also insist that it is God's will that we all be well, that God doesn't seem to have any good purpose of suffering. But is our being free of illness or disability a major concern of God?

From where I sit, I see that, if anything, God is on the side of holiness. You see, health is not the issue in the Epistles; holiness is.

Difficult as it may be, we must come to realize that, from God's perspective, there is something far more important than physical healing. He is quite willing to sacrifice our physical well-being for our spiritual well-being. J. Sidlow Baxter is correct when he says that "in the divinely permitted scheme of things there is truly a use for sickness."[1]

Despite a lot of study (and I confess, some wishful thinking regarding my own physical problems), I find no clear teaching in the Bible that it is always God's will to heal or that God hates sickness as much as he hates sin. To the contrary, the Scripture instructs us that sickness and suffering play a vital role in God's plan to mature and deepen our walk with him. Philip Yancey writes, "It is never clear to us how suffering and evil can be transformed into a cause of celebration. But that is what we are asked to believe."[2]

A Teaching with Harmful Side Effects

The widespread teaching that God is on the side of health and always wants us to be well not only lacks biblical support, but it contains some harmful side effects. Here are some that have become obvious to me as I travel and interact with fellow Christians.

The Teaching Is Dangerous

Not all teachers of atonement healing condemn the use of medicine and doctors, but some do. This has led to the tragic and unnecessary deaths of some of their followers. Our local newspaper carried the story of a couple who were convicted of reckless homicide and child neglect in the death of their nine-month-old daughter, who died of an untreated brain infection. The couple claimed they were practicing the teachings of the Bible by withholding medical treatment from their child.

Several years ago a pastor friend died unnecessarily because he fell into this false teaching and refused medical treatment. His illness was treatable and curable, but he died while like-minded friends knelt around his bed praising God for his healing.

One healing minister advises his followers that when the familiar TV spot about "Warning Signs of Breast Cancer" appears, a woman should refuse to watch it. Even looking for signs of cancer would give the Devil permission, which he did not have before, to afflict her with breast cancer. Such counsel is at best irresponsible; at its worst, it's deadly.

It Adds Guilt to Grief

Once, while I was conducting a conference in their church, a couple came to me with an unbearable burden. Their child had died recently. That is enough burden for any parent to bear, but the unbearable burden was the guilt laid on them by friends who told them their child could have been healed if they had had enough faith. I encounter this situation all the time. Would a *true* friend ever say something like that to grieving parents?

When we lose a loved one, we are always besieged by guilt. "Could I have done more?" "Why didn't I act sooner?" That is a natural part of the grieving process. Guilt weighs heavier, cuts deeper, and stays longer than any other grieving emotion. It derails the mind off the tracks of logic, and we feel responsible for things over which we have little control.

It Raises False Hopes

Many a pastor, after the traveling faith healer has left for another town and the TV preacher has gone off the air, is left with the task of patching up the lives of sick church members whose faith has been crippled by the false hopes of guaranteed healing.

Wade Boggs says, "It is probable that this spiritual and mental tragedy overshadows the physical, for no disappointment can equal the disappointment of a broken faith in the promises of God. It is a very serious thing to raise the hopes of multitudes of sick people with assurances that God will always reward true faith by healing diseases and then to lead the great majority of these people through disillusionment to despair."[3]

It Promotes Self-Condemnation

Closely related to guilt is self-condemnation. Guilt usually surfaces when I couldn't acquire or contribute to another person's healing. Self-condemnation comes when that person is *me*.

When people are assured that healing is their right and inheritance, and yet they cannot obtain this healing, the door is flung open for self-condemnation. "What's wrong with me?" they ask. "Why can't I be healed?" Their failure to receive healing seems to them irrefutable evidence that something is wrong with them. And if these sick people are hard-core believers in atonement healing, it may never occur to them that the teaching might be wrong; they immediately assume the fault lies with them. And this self-condemnation is often aided by sincere but misguided friends who insist there must be some lack of faith or secret sin the sufferers haven't confessed.

In their book *Death and the Caring Community*, Larry Richards and Paul Johnson say,

> We want to be extremely careful in ministering to the . . . ill that we never suggest the illness or its progress their fault. . . . When the person who is ill is not healed, the waves of guilt wash back, and God appears to be a distant, disapproving tyrant who withholds love because His child has failed to perform up to His demanding standards.
>
> The tragedy of this approach to healing is that, just when the believer most needs assurance of God's love and presence, others distort God into a completely different Person than He is. At a time when the individual feels most weak, and most in need of grace to help, this approach demands great

strength as the price of acceptance and love. How
good to know that God is not that kind of Person.[4]

It Prevents God from Ministering to Us through Our Sickness

If we believe that sickness is always contrary to the will of
God, then we will be occupied solely with getting rid of it. This
"theology of escape" closes our mind to any thought that God
might use it for good. Rather than profiting from our illness, we
will burrow ourselves into deeper misery, enlarging our capacity
to feel every needle in the haystack of pain and discomfort. Such
a reaction to sickness makes us incapable of understanding what
Madame Guyon meant when she said, "Ah, if you knew what
peace there is in accepted sorrow." Sometimes God uses the sickness of the body to heal the sickness of the soul.

Just this morning my wife and I visited with a longtime friend.
The past year delivered a tragic blow to her and her family. Cancer
having been discovered in her body, she has been in and out of
the hospital, and the prognosis is not good. Today was one of the
few days she felt like getting out of the house. As we talked, she
told of lying in the hospital looking for a promise from the Lord
that would assure her everything was going to be all right. But
the statement that she kept finding over and over was, "Your eyes
shall see the King."

"That was not the kind of promise I was looking for," she said,
tears filling her eyes. "But I came to realize that this was the best
promise of all." And then she said, *"This has been the best year of
my life."*

There is no doubt in my mind that our friend clings to the
hope for a miraculous healing, but in the meantime she has
allowed God to minister to her through her suffering.

It Destroys Compassion for Those Who Are Hurting

The teaching that God always wants us well, if unrestrained, produces a pharisaic, judgmental attitude that curdles the milk of human kindness.

A pastor in Tennessee had led his church for many years to believe in "healing on demand." And then his little boy developed diabetes. The father, standing in faith that God would heal the child without intervention from physicians or medicine, kept his son away from them. The boy steadily worsened. Finally, a fellow pastor challenged him: "Your little boy is going to die if you don't get help right away."

It was no easy battle for the pastor. Finally, on a Sunday morning he stood before his congregation and revealed for the first time his boy's illness and his decision to seek medical help. The response of the church? They fired him on the spot, accusing him of hidden sin. Is this what Paul meant when he said we should "bear one another's burdens" (Gal. 6:2)?

The husband of one of our dearest friends (I had married them twenty years earlier) suddenly found himself in the hospital dying rapidly from a malignant brain tumor. One day a woman was sent to his wife by a healing evangelist whom the wife had supported financially. With the confidence of the unhurt, she piously announced that the evangelist had received a word from God for her. Her husband was dying because of the wife's lack of faith; not only must she correct her faulty faith, she must immediately remove her husband from the hospital, for there were demons of death working there.

Now I will give the messenger the benefit of the doubt and assume she meant well, thinking she was on a spiritual mission. But how much more would a kind word, a gentle hand on the shoulder, and a shared tear have meant to this wife?

Perhaps these were the kinds of people Shakespeare had in mind when he said, "He jests at scars who never felt a wound."

It Forces Us to Concoct Excuses for Failure

When you lead someone to Christ, it is not always easy to tell whether the person's profession of faith was genuine or spurious. But in the matter of healing, failures are pretty easily identified, especially if the patient dies. Have you ever wondered why so many continue to believe in "healing for all" in the light of so many failures? Always there seems to be an explanation: Not enough faith or unconfessed sin are two of the most frequent reasons given. Gaining in popularity is another explanation that I think needs to be dealt with. It is the claim of "perfect" or "complete" healing.

This excuse is used when a person for whom healing has been claimed dies. "Praise God, he has received perfect healing!" is the response I hear most often. Four points need to be noted.

First, the Bible never speaks of death as healing, perfect or otherwise. Death is still considered by the Bible as an enemy, the last enemy to be destroyed. And while the Scriptures may refer to a Christian's death as falling asleep, it never describes it as healing. If a person succumbs to a disease, he has not been healed, he has died! The terms *perfect healing* and *complete healing* are creations of faith healers, not Scripture writers.

Second, if death is "perfect healing" then why isn't this what we pray for in the first place? Surely we want that which is "perfect" and "complete." So why not just come right out and pray for the person to die?

Third, dying is not what we have in mind when we pray for healing. The whole point of praying for healing is that the person will not die. To say then that death is "perfect healing" is a clear contradiction. The phrase is a loophole that a lawyer would die for, an escape clause to save face when failure strikes.

Finally, if death is "real," "perfect," or "complete" healing, then why bother to pray at all? If the person has lung cancer, the disease will "heal" him soon enough, without our prayers.

No, much as we might wish it so because suffering is painful, God does not always want us well. There are times when he uses sickness, suffering, and death to help us draw closer to him, to learn to trust him more, to acknowledge that he is sovereign, and to grow in faith that, even though we may not be able to see it with our earthly sight, he indeed has greater good in store.

PART THREE

Finding God's Good in Suffering

Where the seen and the unseen copulate
they sire a child named mystery.
—Calvin Miller, *An Overture to Light*

Let it come as it will and don't be afraid, God does not
leave us Comfortless. So let the evening come.
—Jane Kenyon, *Let Evening Come*

CHAPTER 15

Divine Temple or Clay Pot?

Christians Experience Pain Like Everyone Else but with One Redeeming Difference

NOT LONG AGO I VISITED with a delightful Christian who, when we said our good-byes, fired this parting shot: "Love God! Hate sin! *And watch out for trucks!*"

Run into any trucks lately on the road of life? As Christians we sometimes tend to think that if we love God and hate sin, we don't need to watch out for trucks. It's good to be reminded that even though we are God's children, our bodies are still human and subject to the dangers of everyday living.

After I presented a series of lectures on the subject of healing, a member of the congregation asked me what effect did I believe my teaching would have on the sick. In response to him I said that I hoped to present a proper biblical view of the topic that will encourage people to face sickness with the right attitude and understanding—and to pray in a scriptural manner. Being biblical and balanced are my primary concerns. To accomplish this, I think it is essential we have a biblical view of the human body.

Impact of the Fall

To start, it's important to understand that . . . the body took a direct hit from the fall and is now subject to the processes of death and decay.

In other words, "Watch out for trucks!"

Paul describes believers as clay jars (see 2 Cor. 4:7 NIV). But the jars have been cracked by the fall. Christians are cracked pots. Describing the results of the fall, Claus Westermann points out, "The remarkable fact is that a person's work is always joined in some way with toil, trouble, even with sweat and thorns."[1] Thorns and thistles inhabit every field of work; harvest demands sweat.

"Till you return to the ground" (Gen. 3:19). Man must labor till he dies. This labor never ends; it is with us till we die. Even in retirement, this toil remains with us. The toil is there long after the job is finished. You may be sailing the South Seas on a sixty-foot yacht or enjoying retirement in a condo on Florida's beaches, but the toil will still be there. "In their origin and in their destiny human beings belong to the dust. Everything noble and great that can be said of a person and of one's capabilities must be circumscribed by this limit which has been set to all that is human."[2]

The body is not as God created it. Like a bombed-out building, traces of the original image remain, but it has been terribly marred. Though we may be new creatures in Christ, we remain part of the human situation. We still are partakers of human nature, and if cut, we bleed.

The New Testament, therefore, views our present salvation as primarily confined to the spiritual part of man. Consider the following passages from Paul's letters:

Therefore we do not lose heart, but though our
outer man is decaying, yet our inner man is being
renewed day by day. (2 Cor. 4:16)

For indeed while we are in this tent, we groan,
being burdened, because we do not want to be
unclothed but to be clothed, so that what is mortal
may be swallowed up by life. (2 Cor. 5:4)

For our citizenship is in heaven, from which
also we eagerly wait for a Savior, the Lord Jesus
Christ; who will transform the body of our humble
state into conformity with the body of His glory,
by the exertion of the power that He has even to
subject all things to Himself. (Phil. 3:20–21)

For the creation was subjected to futility, not
willingly, but because of Him who subjected it, in
hope that the creation itself also will be set free
from its slavery to corruption into the freedom of
the glory of the children of God. For we know that
the whole creation groans and suffers the pains of
childbirth together until now. And not only this,
but also we ourselves, having the first fruits of the
Spirit, even we ourselves groan within ourselves,
waiting eagerly for our adoption as sons, the
redemption of our body. (Rom. 8:20–23)

The body of the Christian does not differ physically from
that of the non-Christian. No special immunity is granted to us,
no charmed existence bestowed upon us. Atonement healing is
popular because it appeals to the universal desire to transcend the

fragile humanity of mere mortals. But Christians experience pain like everyone else, with this redeeming difference: the knowledge that our suffering is part of God's ministry in us. James writes, "Consider it all joy, my brethren, when you encounter various trials, knowing that the testing of your faith produces endurance. And let endurance have its perfect result, so that you may be perfect and complete, lacking in nothing" (James 1:2–4).

I was amazed at a discovery I made in a well-known verse of Scripture, a verse I had read many times and preached on often. It's 1 Corinthians 10:13: "No temptation has overtaken you but such as is common to man; and God is faithful, who will not allow you to be tempted beyond what you are able, but with the temptation will provide the way of escape also, so that you will be able to endure it."

Endure it! I thought we were going to *escape it!* Hmm, this God doesn't think the way I do. To me, escaping is escaping, but to God you escape it when you are able to endure it. We escape it in the sense that it does not hold us prisoner, we are not enslaved to the trial. To escape it doesn't mean we don't feel the pain and pressure of it.

Not exemption from the trials, but escape through endurance. Granted to the believer are heavenly resources that enable him to turn his suffering into victory and glory. Not only that, we have the assurance of his presence and comfort.

Promise of Redemption

As a child on Christmas morning discovers that there is yet one more gift under the tree—and it is the best, for the believer the best is yet to be! While the cross of Christ took away our sins, it did not remove sin's present consequences. Healing may be in the atonement, as many insist, but the truth is we have not yet experienced all that the atonement made available to us. The body is yet to be redeemed.

"Then comes the end, when He hands over the kingdom to the God and Father, when He has abolished all rule and authority and power" (1 Cor. 15:24).

Peter writes of this coming redemption, saying that we "are protected by the power of God through faith for a salvation ready to be revealed in the last time . . . so that . . . your faith . . . may be found to result in praise and glory and honor at the revelation of Jesus Christ . . . Therefore, prepare your minds for action, keep sober in spirit, fix your hope completely on the grace to be brought to you at the revelation of Jesus Christ" (1 Pet. 1:5, 7, 13).

And to me one of the most precious promises in the Bible is "And He will wipe away every tear from their eyes; and there will no longer be any death; there will no longer by any mourning, or crying, or pain; the first things have passed away" (Rev. 21:4).

The apostle here uses the future tense when he says there will be no more death, mourning, crying, or pain. *Pain* is a kind of catchall word in Greek and indicates laborious toil, distress, affliction, and pain of any sort.

The phrase "the first things have passed away" summarizes what has just been said. "First" or "former things" (KJV) refer to the consequences of sin entering the world. He makes it clear that not only will the old heaven and earth pass away but all the marring details that belong to it. In other words, these things that we seek to be rid of in the here and now will not be taken away until the then and there. But until then, regardless of how great our faith or how intense our praying, there is going to be sorrow, crying, and pain on the earth.

This unholy trinity—sorrow, crying, and pain—goose-step through our life as if lords of the earth. No amount of locks, laws, or alarms can secure the doors of our life from these loathsome intruders. But the best is yet to be! T. DeWitt Talmadge writes,

> But I have a glad sound for every hospital, for every sick room, for every lifelong invalid, for every broken heart, "There shall be no more pain." No crepe floats from the door of that blissful residence. He whose foot touches that pavement becomes an athlete. The first kiss of the summer will take the wrinkles from the old man's cheeks. The first flash of the throne will scatter the darkness of those who were born blind.[3]

One day God himself shall wipe away every tear (the Greek reads literally, "every *single* tear") from our eyes. On that day there won't be a damp eye in the place.

But all that is yet to come. The "former things" are not former yet. God has a sovereign purpose for allowing us to endure suffering.

Our Bodies for His Glory

The body belongs to God and should be consecrated to his glory. Therefore to the Corinthians, whose carnality was rooted in the belief that their bodies were theirs to do with as they pleased, Paul wrote, "The body is . . . for the Lord, and the Lord is for the body" (1 Cor. 6:13).

A carnal Christian is one who believes he has a right to his own body. The cure for carnality is to recognize that your body is the Lord's. "Or do you not know that your body is a temple of the Holy Spirit . . . and that you are not your own? For you have been bought with a price." And then Paul drives home the logical conclusion: "Therefore glorify God in your body" (1 Cor. 6:19–20).

Having been bought and paid for by the blood of Christ, Paul urged the Roman Christians "to present your bodies a living and holy sacrifice" (Rom. 12:1).

The operative word in these and similar verses is "glorify." Since our bodies belong to him by right of redemption, they are to be used exclusively for his glory. It is significant that in all these exhortations there is not a single promise that if the believer obeys, he will be immune from sickness or guaranteed bodily healing. On the contrary, Paul says that he himself is "always carrying about in the body the dying of Jesus . . . constantly being delivered over to death for Jesus' sake" (2 Cor. 4:10–11). The reason for this is "that the life of Jesus also may be manifested in our body" (v. 10), and "that the life of Jesus also may be manifested in our mortal flesh" (v. 11). When the shadow of martyrdom passed over Paul's head, he said that his earnest expectation was that "Christ will even now, as always, be exalted in my body, whether by life or by death" (Phil. 1:20).

For us twenty-first-century believers, living and dying are the great issues. We cling to life as if there were no afterlife; we shun death at all costs. But to the great apostle, living and dying were secondary matters; the main thing was Christ being magnified in his body.

The body is God's magnifying glass through which Jesus, invisible to the world, is made conspicuous. Jesus is the telescope through which, distant and inaccessible to the world, he is brought near. A Christian's body is the instrument God uses to demonstrate Christ's greatness and nearness. Sometimes this can best be accomplished through sickness, sometimes through healing. But sickness or healing is of secondary importance. Christ is to be magnified in everything. To God this is more precious than health or healing.

It is God's way to use sickness and affliction for his glory. On hearing that Lazarus was sick, Jesus said, "This sickness is not to end in death, but for the glory of God, so that the son of God may be glorified by it" (John 11:4). Now watch it: Jesus said, "This sickness is not to end in death." *But Lazarus died!* Did Jesus make a bad call on that one? Was he mistaken? It would seem so. But Jesus did not actually say that Lazarus would not die. He said, "This sickness is not *unto* death."

The Greek construction is an unusual one and literally translated is, "This sickness is not with a view to death." In other words, while Lazarus would die, the purpose of the sickness was not death, but the glory of God. The purpose of some sickness is death, but not this one. It was an opportunity for God to display his works; therefore, God allowed Lazarus to die. Even though the illness ended in death, it was not a dangerous sickness.

To deny that God often uses sickness to accomplish his purpose is to cast shadows upon some of the greatest names in church history, saints like Richard Baxter, Madame Guyon, David Brainerd, George Matheson, Francis Ridley Havergal, Amy Carmichael, Fanny J. Crosby, Annie Johnson Flint, Joni Eareckson Tada—men and women whose physical suffering unveiled to the world a God of abundant sufficiency. Imagine how impoverished the church would be without the hymns, poems, sermons, works of art, and testimonies produced by sickness and suffering.

Concerning the promises of God, we do well to remember that whatever promises he makes and to whomever he makes them, he never does so at the expense of his sovereignty over our lives. The Bible says that God takes note of every sparrow that falls. Wonderful promise. But notice: The sparrow *does* fall. Psalm 23 assures us that "though I walk through the valley of the shadow of death, I will fear no evil" (v. 4). It doesn't say that we won't face or feel the evil. We must still walk through the valley. Richards and Johnson write,

> On the other hand we want to affirm that God can heal . . . While God normally works through natural processes . . . God is not under bondage to natural law.
>
> On the other hand, we want to be just as clear in stating that God does not limit His own freedom to the amount or quality of a human being's "faith." It is a complete misunderstanding of faith to view it as a work that can compel God to act according to our will.[4]

Often when the purpose of suffering has been achieved, such as an increase of faith or the humbling of the saint or the equipping of the believer to sympathetically minister to others, the malady may be lifted.

Charles Spurgeon said, "I venture to say that the greatest gift God can give us is health, *with the exception of sickness.* Sickness has frequently been of more use to the saints of God than health has."

But the well-known bottom line is, which is more important: our physical well-being or God's glory? Our answer will reveal the depth of our knowledge of God.

CHAPTER 16

Praying for the Sick

What You Do Not Receive,
You Do Not Require

I DREADED THE VISIT.

Of course, I always dreaded visiting the children's hospital. The sight of small twisted bodies, young faces with the pallor of death from cancer and leukemia, bald and swollen heads, was almost more than I could bear.

I was not long out of seminary, and the infant son of a young couple in the church where I was pastor had become suddenly and mysteriously ill. After a few days he was hospitalized in serious condition. Tests were run but revealed nothing. The doctors were stumped. The baby's fever had risen to such a height that brain damage and even death was the prognosis. I visited the despairing parents every day in the child's hospital room, trying to comfort them as best I could. The visits always concluded with prayer. One day as we gathered around the child's bed to pray, a strange thing happened. I was suddenly overcome with the presence of God; I *knew* God wanted to heal this child. I don't know how I knew, I just knew. Never had I been as certain of anything in my life.

As we prayed, I placed my hand on the baby's burning head and asked God to heal him and thanked him for doing it. Within a couple of days the baby was released from the hospital, healed.

On another occasion I was summoned to Parkland Hospital in Dallas. A member of our church had been admitted with two seriously diseased kidneys. His wife called and asked if I would visit him.

When I arrived in ICU, I saw my church member (who rarely attended church) hooked up to the dialysis machine. I don't think I've ever seen such a frightened man. His life expectancy, according to the doctors, was just a matter of weeks. When he saw me, he started begging me to pray for him and promising that if God healed him, he would commit himself totally to Christ and serve him fully.

I knew that you don't negotiate with God and that God is not impressed with our promises. Yet as I stood beside this man's bed, I *knew* that God would heal him, in spite of his backslidden ways. And I thought, *Who knows, this may really turn his life around.* Placing my hand on his head, I prayed that God would intervene and heal him of his disease. When I finished praying, I told him that God had heard our prayers and that he would be all right. Torrents of thanks and promises gushed from his mouth. The last thing he said as I left the room was, "I'll be in church the first Sunday I am out of here."

God did heal him, and within a few days he was released from the hospital. The first Sunday came, but he didn't show. Nor did he come the second or third Sunday. Then I sensed God giving me a strange message to go to this man's house, read a passage of Scripture, and leave.

I was nervous as I sat in his living room. I had never done anything like this before.

"Bill," I said, "God has sent me here with a message for you."

He sat quietly as I opened my Bible to John 5 and read about the man who was healed at Bethesda. Then I came to the message of verse 14: "Afterward Jesus found him in the temple and said to him, 'Behold, you have become well; do not sin anymore, *so that nothing worse happens to you.*'" I got up to leave and said, "Bill, God has not done his worst yet."

I never saw him again. Not long after that the family moved away. As far as I know, Bill never kept a single promise he made to God. I learned one thing from that experience—miracles do not make you spiritual (see rule 4 in chapter 10).

Since then there have been a number of other similar incidents. On those occasions when it does happen, I don't sweat and strain to believe God for healing; it's easy for me to believe. And it is easy because it is a gift, a gift imparted by God to my heart that makes possible "the prayer of faith."

But there have been more times when I have struggled to believe, fasted, and prayed for someone's healing, but the healing did not come. Often our whole church has fasted and prayed and believed and claimed—and the healing did not come. Why is that?

J. Sidlow Baxter writes, "If special faith must be the agent which grasps and brings the healing, then God will inspire such faith. The only instances (whether few or many) in which such faith is *not* imparted are those in which God designs some important spiritual ministry through permitted sickness . . . I have known sick Christians to be healed, not of their sickness, but by it."[1] If the sickness should be a means of chastening, when the chastening has accomplished its refining work, God may see fit to heal.

Whatever the specific reason for some affliction, I believe we should always (unless definitely impressed otherwise) pray for healing, leaving the final disposition of the matter with God. It is always fitting to pray for what we believe is a legitimate need.

Of course, God may show us that what we consider a need is not one at all. But it's safe to say that if healing is a God-recognized need, we will be healed. Based on Philippians 4:19, "And my God will supply all your needs according to His riches in glory in Christ Jesus," a motto of my life is, What you do not receive, you do not require.

Legitimate versus Imagined Needs

The trick is discerning between a *legitimate* need and an *imagined* need. The child of God is no more qualified to decide what is best for him in spiritual matters than an earthly child is in material matters.

Every parent has fought this battle time and again with his children. Frequently the child interprets the actions of the parents as unfair and uncaring, when in fact they are acts of love. The psalmist declares, "No good thing does He withhold from those who walk uprightly" (84:11). If healing is best for us, God will not withhold it. So even as we pray for healing, we should acknowledge that only our heavenly Father knows what we truly need, and that if he chooses not to bestow the desired cure, it is because he has something infinitely better.

The Next Step

If we still are not healed after having done all we know to do, the next step is to accept our affliction as a part of God's ongoing ministry in us. To God, character is far more precious than comfort. He often uses uncomfortable circumstances to change our character. When the circumstances have fulfilled their task, then God may change the circumstances. But if he doesn't, it will be all right because our character will have been so changed that we will be able to live with uncomfortable circumstances. Paul's thorn-in-the-flesh experience is a perfect example of changed character rejoicing in the midst of unchanged circumstances. The authors of *Death and the Caring Community* tell us:

> While death is inevitable for all except the final generation (1 Thessalonians 4:13–18), the date of any individual's death is not. As the first "whys" are asked, the caring community can and should gather around the individual with prayer to God for healing . . . It is always appropriate to bring needs to God . . . God may choose to answer the prayer for healing . . . or God may choose not to intervene. And then the individual and the community will find the grace to affirm His faithfulness in spite of the apparent silence.[2]

In Philippians 4:6–7, Paul tells us not to worry about anything but to pray about everything. He doesn't promise that in doing so, God will remove the worrisome thing. He does promise us that the peace of Christ will guard our hearts and minds.

What about James 5:13–15?

Often when we think of praying for healing, James 5:13–15 immediately springs to mind. We automatically associate it with the familiar scenes in some churches and on some religious telecast in which sick folk stream to the altar to receive anointing and prayer. Some healing ministries are based wholly on this difficult and controversial passage. It is one, therefore, that demands careful investigation.

Verse 15 states, "The prayer of faith shall save the sick" (KJV). Commenting on this verse, Curtis Vaughn writes, "The fact that the promise is stated in unconditional terms raises a problem, for it is obvious that believing prayer does not always result in bodily healing."[3]

The problem is real, for believing prayer *does not* always result in healing. Who can doubt the faith of those who believe to the extent that they are willing to let their children die rather than receive medical help? Death in the face of such unwavering and tenacious faith demands that we ask, "How much faith does it take?"

An Overview

But above all, my brethren, do not swear, either by heaven or by earth or with any other oath; but your yes is to be yes, and your no, no, so that you may not fall under judgment.

Is anyone among you suffering? Then he must pray. Is anyone cheerful? He is so to sing praises.

Is anyone among you sick? Then he must call for the elders of the church and they are to pray over him, anointing him with oil in the name of the Lord; and the prayer offered in faith will restore the one who is sick, and the Lord will raise him up, and if he has committed sins, they will be forgiven him. (James 5:12–15)

You will notice that I began with verse 12; I believe the admonition against swearing leads James into the following verses. Alfred Plummer states, "Oaths are not the right way of expressing one's feelings, however strong they may be, and of whatever kind they may be. There is, however, no need to stifle such feelings, or to pretend to the world that we have no emotions."[4] Christians need a fail-safe system to keep from wrongly expressing their feelings. "This safe-guard is clearly indicated by the rules here laid down by St. James. Let the expression of strongly excited feelings be an act of worship . . . By the very act in which we exhibit our emotions we protect ourselves from the evil which they might produce."[5]

James selects three examples of Christian emotional experiences and suggests the proper expression of each:

Is anyone suffering? (the emotion): Let him pray (the expression).

Is anyone cheerful? (the emotion): Let him sing praises (the expression).

Is anyone sick? (the emotion): Let him call the elders (the expression).

The section ends with the third example, calling for the elders to pray over the sick person. This leads James to make the statement in verse 15 about the prayer of faith raising the sick believer.

The key to understanding this passage is to recognize that verses 14 and 15 need to be separated in our thinking, for James is saying two different things. He is saying (1) that a sick believer should call for the elders of the church to pray over him, and (2) that the prayer of faith will raise the sick. He is not saying that every time the elders pray over a sick believer, anointing him with oil, healing will occur. What he is saying is this: If we're sick, let us call for the elders to pray over us *and* in those instances where the prayer of faith is offered, the sick person will be raised up.

Why this view? Because the words used for *prayer* and *sick* are different in both verses. Let's compare them.

Verse 14: The Greek word for sick is *astheneo*, which means to be sick, feeble, or weak. It is used in Acts 20:35 to indicate being in need economically.[6]

"And let them *pray*" translates the verb form of the Greek word *proseuchomai*, the most frequent word for prayer to God; it is used eighty-seven times in the New Testament.

Verse 15: Here the word for sick is *kamno*, found only three times in the New Testament, the word meaning to be weary, fatigued. It can also indicate someone who is hopelessly ill and wasting away. "In the physical realm the word means 'hopelessly sick;' that is, sick to the point that death was imminent. Frequently it described those who were dead."[7]

"And the prayer offered in faith [or more correctly, *the prayer of faith*]" translates a word for prayer that is employed only three times in the New Testament, *eukee*. And only in James is it translated *prayer*. In Acts 18:18 and Acts 21:23, it is rendered *vow*; thus, it is more than a prayer in the sense of prayer in verse 14. It is a prayer comprising a vow.

It is difficult to believe that James, writing under the guidance of the Holy Spirit, would make such obvious changes in words without a specific reason. Was it because he was speaking of two different, though related, cases?

A Closer Look

Several points deserve mention. We'll start with verse 14.

1. It is the sick person who calls for the elders. The elders do not seek out the sick and initiate the contact. I will not dogmatically say that it is scripturally incorrect for

healing ministers to travel the country, holding anointing services. But such practice cannot honestly be based on James 5:14, for this is not at all what the writer has in mind. The man in verse 14 is too sick, too weak, and too weary to attend services. His condition is such that the elders must come to him—at his invitation.

2. The elders are to pray over the sick believer, "having anointed him with oil." Common in the ancient world, it is an enigma to ours, this anointing with oil. No one can say with certainty how James intends the oil to function. It could have been as *medicine*. To the ancients, oil, especially olive oil, was believed to possess certain curative powers. Galen refers to oil as "the best of all remedies for paralysis." The Jewish rabbis were known to use oil when visiting the sick, and the Good Samaritan applied oil and wine to the wounds of the man attacked by robbers (see Luke 10:34).

Some see oil as a *symbol* of the Holy Spirit. Oil is frequently used in the Bible as a symbol of the Spirit, and anointing the sick with oil would be a recognition of the Spirit's power to drive out illness. Others see oil as *an aid to faith*. Still others believe the entire ritual was confined to apostolic times.

But whatever the significance of the oil in James, the important point is that the *Lord* raises up the sick person, not the anointing of the oil or the prayers of the elders. It would be wrong to pattern all healing efforts after the procedure in James. As we have already seen in previous chapters, Jesus and his disciples did not limit themselves to any one method or procedure in healing. James is simply mentioning *one* way to do it.

Not surprisingly, there is much disagreement about present-day application of this passage. Many insist that the whole procedure ended with the close of the apostolic era. They may be right but, personally, I find nothing unscriptural about a seriously ill Christian calling for the elders of the church to pray for him. If the sick person believes such prayer and anointing would encourage his faith and honor the Lord, I would never deny him the right to do it.

The Prayer of Faith

Let's move now to verse 15. Two important points need to be made as we examine this verse. (1) Concerning the phrase "the prayer of faith": Does James mean that when we pray for healing, the healing will come if we truly believe? It has already been noted that believing in prayer *does not* always result in bodily healing. What, then, does James mean?

James, I believe, is referring to a specific kind of prayer, a prayer produced by the divine impartation of faith. In the Greek text there is a definite article before "prayer"—"*the* prayer of faith." The use of the definite article in Greek carries special significance: "The basal function of the Greek article is to point out individual identity."[8]

The prayer of faith is more than praying in faith. It is a special and specific prayer that God enables us to offer by imparting faith for healing. It is a God-infused faith and a God-inspired prayer,

In his classic little book *The Bible and the Body*, Rowland V. Bingham says,

> The question of whether God intends to heal along natural or supernatural lines will be generally indicated in the consciousness of those called in to pray. God sometimes moves out in the faith that is able to claim instantaneous healing,

and, when such an inspired prayer is offered, the answer immediately comes, and all other means are unnecessary. . . . On the other hand we have been present in meetings where for hours prayer has been made for an afflicted child of God, when they claimed that they were standing in "Atonement ground," and therefore, they insisted that they had the right to claim the healing, and *nothing has moved*, even though they stirred themselves up to most zealous earnestness.[9]

W. D. Evans was for many years pastor of the Sunbridge Road Mission in Bradford, England. Shortly before he retired, I held a series of meetings in his church and heard some of his remarkable experiences with healings. Here's one he shared with me in a letter that illustrates my point:

> My wife was teaching at a local school. One day she came home with a strange request. A member of her staff had been longing for a baby for many years but medically there was little hope. She and her husband asked if I would pray that Jesus, the Lord of Life, would give them a child.
>
> The request came on a Thursday; Thursday evenings was my Bible school, so I asked the school to pray with me. Each Thursday for about three months we prayed until we heard the wonderful news that Margaret was pregnant.
>
> Later that year I was asked to go to Thailand to preach at a missionary Bible college. It would be a dangerous visit and a costly one so I laid the request before the Lord and asked Him to show me His way, and He did.

Within a few weeks of this request I was visiting a local hospital when a call came over the tannoy system—would I immediately go to the local maternity hospital which was about three miles away. As I went through the hospital door the Lord clearly told me, "This child shall live." At that moment I did not know whose child I was going to see. The sister on the Premature Baby Unit was upset as I had been so long in arriving. The baby was dying. However, I put on a hospital coat, told the sister not to worry, the baby would be fine, and went into the ward. I was asked to name the baby before it died; medically there was no hope. Then I realized it was our "Bible School Baby," arrived far too soon, but I still felt intense joy and certainty in this tiny life.

The nurse later apologized to the parents—she felt I was drunk, I was so happy about the baby. When I saw the mother she presumed her baby was dead. My reply was, "The Lord did not answer our prayer just to take her away at birth. She will be well." We prayed a prayer of thanksgiving—I went off to Thailand, praising the Lord for showing me His greatness and power.

Susan Elizabeth is now eleven years old and absolutely beautiful.

Sick of Sin

"And if he has committed sins, they will be forgiven him." The second crucial point in verse 15 is this: (2) James forges a significant link between sickness and sin in this verse. He follows through in the next verse: "therefore confess your sins to one another, and pray for one another so that you may be healed. The effective prayer of a righteous man can accomplish much" (v. 16).

When in verse 15 James says, "And if he has committed sins," we know he is not considering that the man in question is sinless. Where our sinning is concerned, there is no "if" about it.

No, James isn't speaking in general terms, implying this sick fellow may be free of sin. In the light of the context, he means, "If he has sinned in such a way as to have brought this sickness upon him." The Greek word *committed* is a perfect active subjective (this is for lawyers, doctors, and writers of business letters, insurance policies, and IRS instructions). What it means is that there exists the possibility—no, the probability—that the sickness was caused by sin. Curtis Vaughn points out, "These words suggest that illness in some cases may be due to the sin of the sufferer. In such a case, the effecting of a miraculous cure would be a clear indication that the sins of the afflicted person were forgiven."[10]

The critical point to consider here is the obvious link between sickness and sin. Thus the possible conclusion: All that James teaches here about praying for the sick applies only to the sickness caused by sin. Following the rule of interpretation that tells us to interpret every text in the light of its context, we have more than enough room to accommodate that conclusion.

Some Guidelines for Praying for Healing

After our trek through the jungle of James 5:13–15, I want to suggest some guidelines for praying for the sick. These are not rules, for there are no fixed and final rules in this matter. In the final analysis we "just go at it" the best we know, trusting God to understand our hearts and to forgive any violations of protocol.

1. Be honest about your condition—with yourself, others, and God. You may be accused of negative thinking, but remember: There's a fine line between positive confession and plain old lying. It's okay to be sick.
2. Pray and ask God for guidance in your praying.
3. Pray for God's healing.
4. Use the best medical help available.
5. Confess your sins. If you have offended or sinned against anyone, make it right and seek reconciliation.
6. Pray that you will learn well all that God wants to teach you by this illness.
7. Do not put God to the test by demanding that he heal you.
8. Do not judge God on the basis of your physical condition.
9. Remember that at the heart of Christianity stands a cross, and pray that God will use your suffering as a means of bringing others to him.
10. When you don't know what to pray, pray, "Father, glorify Your name" (John 12:28).

But if, after all this, God says no, what are we to do?

CHAPTER 17

When God Says No

God Often Draws Outside the Lines
We Have Drawn for Him

GOD HAS NOT ANSWERED SOME of my biggest prayers. I know the disappointment of God saying no when I thought he would say yes.

While God had answered my prayer for healing in several non-family situations, my mother died of cancer at age sixty in spite of my earnest prayer and those of many others. My oldest son, suffering from manic depression, took his life at age eighteen. We weren't "hoping" God would heal him. We *knew* that he would. He had given us a promise that Kaye kept stuck to the refrigerator. My father-in-law died of cancer at age sixty-two. In 1990, my father died of cancer.

In the matter of healing there is one question that plagues everyone, and to which there is no satisfying answer: Why does God heal some and not others?

Eddie and Michele Rasnake are dear friends and staff members at the Woodland Park Baptist Church in Chattanooga,

Tennessee. Shortly after giving birth to her fourth child, Michele began to experience a searing, gripping pain in her back that became unbearable. On October 8, 1992, this beautiful thirty-year-old wife and mother learned that she had non-Hodgkins T-cell lymphoma. It was present in her breasts, chest, shoulder, chin, liver, arm, three places on her spine, and in the pelvis—an aggressive, stage four cancer. The doctors gave her a 20- to 40-percent chance of survival. In reality, this was a death sentence.

Tests and treatments left her in greater pain. She had a violent reaction to a blood transfusion. The valley grew deeper every day. On a day when those close to her prayed and fasted for her healing, Michele only got worse. She was packed in ice because of fever. Then she developed chemical meningitis from the chemotherapy treatments. The pain from headaches caused violent jerking of her head every couple of minutes. The doctors gave her morphine for the pain and two hours later they doubled the dose.

"At the lowest points," Eddie recalls, "all we knew to do was to read the Psalms. At one point we read the Psalms for nearly two hours *until we got things back into perspective*" (emphasis added). A lawyer was called in to set their legal affairs in order. "I was at the point of beginning to grapple with the reality that she might not make it," says Eddie. An irregular heartbeat created a new concern.

Throughout all this God kept calling Eddie and Michele back to the Word. One Scripture that became very meaningful for Michele was Revelation 4:8, "Holy, holy, holy is the Lord God, the Almighty, who was and who is and who is to come."

Another biopsy on March 9, 1993, still showed cancer present on the spine. Further testing was recommended, plus a second biopsy. The night before the second biopsy, Michele sought the Lord and he was faithful.

"I felt," says Michele, "as if I had gone as far as I could go, that I had taken as much as I could take. I joked to Eddie that if he got up and the van was gone, not to come looking for me.

"After awhile, in my spirit, I sensed God speaking to me. He said, 'Enough is enough,' and, 'I am going to do a great thing.' What a sense of excitement. I didn't know if God was going to heal me or take me home to be with him or what. *It didn't matter.* The joy and peace of being in the presence of God was wonderful" (emphasis added).

On March 17, 1993, the doctors did a second biopsy. No cancer. Not a cell. Anywhere. A miracle of God placed Michele into remission.

"The greatest miracle is not that he healed me, but that his grace was sufficient for us every step of the way," says Michele. "Eddie always says, 'It is not a story of our great faith; it is the story of God's faithfulness.'"

I talked to Eddie recently and we were discussing the "why some and not others?" of healing. He admitted he didn't understand. "Some of the people who went through the same process we did, didn't make it."

Has God said no to you? What should you do? Go back to chapter 16 and review the guidelines on praying for healing, then pray again. What's to lose? I believe in shooting down every hole—if the Devil is there you'll hit him.

If God still says no, we must recognize that there is no one who can overrule God's decision, no higher court to which we can appeal. And we must conclude that the answer to "Why does God heal some and not others?" is a divine mystery.

The Sovereignty of God

When suddenly confronted with evil, suffering, and death in their own lives, many Christians for the first time entertain serious doubts about God's goodness and his concern over the personal lives of his children. Life has slapped them in the face. They have had a blowout on their road to success. Thus, doubt calls into question not only God's providential care but the validity of prayer, faith, and miracles.

It has long been a tenet of orthodox Christianity that God created the world and rules it with goodness and justice. The Christian faith affirms that God is present and active in the world to carry out his divine purposes and to achieve the divine goal of the fulfillment of all creatures.

Is God active in the world today? Does he intervene in the personal affairs of his people? Does he answer prayer and honor faith?

These were not pressing questions in the early period of Christian thought (nor are they for most of us until we get the bad news). For centuries, believers found, and still do, comfort in the understanding that their lives were overshadowed with divine concern, or what we call "providence." By providence I mean the continuing action of God by which he preserved in existence his creation and guides it toward his intended purpose. But since the seventeenth century, which brought about the Age of Enlightenment, scientific and philosophic thinking has increasingly conflicted with the belief in miracles and providence and the value of prayer.

Augustine (AD 354–430) was perhaps antiquity's greatest theologian. He developed a complex theory of the relation of divine activity to human activity. On the one hand, the divine sovereignty, decree, and providence reign absolute over all of history; God controls all human action. On the other hand, God does act in and through finite causes, both natural and human (e.g., prayer, faith, doctors, and medication).

Thomas Aquinas (1225–1274), an Italian theologian, stated that God can act immediately in the world and also immediately through finite cause. Roman Catholic theology has generally followed this teaching down to the present.

John Calvin (1509–1564) was the father of Reformed doctrine and theology. He asserted that God is in absolute control of the world, that his divine will is the cause of all things. Every drop of rain and the flight of the birds is governed and determined by God's will and plan. God sometimes works through intermediate or secondary causes, sometimes without them, and sometimes in contradiction to them.

The development of modern science in the seventeenth and eighteenth centuries, with its sole interest in natural causes and interpretation of natural events, led to doubts about the reality of divine activity in the world.

The Onset of Deism

Lord Herbert of Cherbury, an English writer of the seventeenth century, is usually seen as the father of Deism. Deism held that God created the world, then left it to run according to inexorable natural laws. It assumed that once creation was complete, God removed himself from it and is no longer personally active in the universe.

The Deist theologians use the classical comparison of God with a watchmaker, who wound up the world once and for all at the beginning and now lets it run without his further involvement.

Of course, this contradicts orthodox Christianity by denying any direct intervention in the natural order by God.

For all practical purposes, Deism is dead, but its legacy continues into this century. Its significance historically has been great, and it still exerts influence on religious thought today. As a result, among liberals and secularists the interpretation of divine activity in the form of "miracle" has almost disappeared. Miracle has become just the religious name for the event.

The majority of conservative Christians, however, still believe that God continues to intervene in his world through miracles, providence, and answers to prayer.

When Doctrine Becomes Personal

Most Christians can watch the news of a military conflict on TV, can contemplate the Holocaust, can read in the newspaper accounts of senseless slaughter and starvation and airplane crashes—and never once question the goodness of God or doubt his power and willingness to intervene on behalf of his people. It is only when evil touches us personally that we are suddenly inundated with doubts and begin asking questions we would never have asked before.

Thus Hans Kung can say, "Many people today have fewer difficulties in believing in a Creator than they have in believing in a Ruler of all things."[1]

In 1981 Rabbi Harold Kushner wrote a best-selling book called *When Bad Things Happen to Good People*, in which he tells how he dealt with his fourteen-year-old son's death of progeria, the horrible rapid-aging disease. A TV interviewer asked him why he wrote the book. He answered that having been a rabbi for many years, he had seen many people die and had conducted countless funerals. But never once had he questioned his belief in God. Only as he watched his innocent son die of that terrible disease did doubt lay siege to his faith.

Kushner writes, "I believe in God. But I do not believe the same things about him that I did years ago when I was growing up, or when I was a theological student. I recognize his limitations."[2] Earlier in the book he says, "God does not want you to be sick or crippled. He didn't make you have this problem, and he doesn't want you to go on having it, but he can't make it go away. That is something which is too hard even for God."[3]

For Kushner the solution was simple: Reduce the sovereign, omnipotent God to a kind but limited one and you can still believe in God and accept the death of an innocent child.

Few orthodox Christians would accept Kushner's solution, but we must admit to doubts when God does not intervene in our own situation. And so the mystery remains. But we can find help if we remember that God suffers with his people.

God Suffers with You

God's willingness and ability to suffer was considered a heretical teaching in the past. But the God we find in the Scriptures is a God who suffers with his people. He not only "delivered the people of Israel from slavery and made them a great nation, but also . . . shared their utter humiliation, powerlessness, and suffering when they were defeated by their enemies and carried off to exile in a foreign land."[4]

An illustration of this suffering God is found in Isaiah 54:7–8. While God tearfully allows judgment to come, he does not abandon those who suffer:

"For a brief moment I forsook you, but with great compassion I will gather you. In an outburst of anger I hid My face from you for a moment, but with everlasting lovingkindness I will have compassion on you," says the LORD your Redeemer.

This is what John Donne must have had in mind when he wrote,

Though thou with clouds of anger do disguise
Thy face; yet through that mask I know those eyes,
Which, though they turn away sometimes,
They never will despise.

God is not an impassive God who stands outside our pain. Rather, through Jesus Christ, as Hebrews 4:15 tells us, he has been tempted in all points as we have, yet without sin. He not only knows how, but actually does *sympathize* with us in our weaknesses. The Greek word means to share the experience with someone. It is not to be understood in a psychological sense, but rather in an existential sense. The exalted One suffers together with the weakness of the one tempted.

Verse 16 says, "*Therefore* let us draw near with confidence to the throne of grace, so that we may receive mercy and find grace to help in time of need." The "therefore" points back to what has been said about our Lord. *Therefore, we can draw near with confidence. Why? Because Jesus knows exactly how we feel, even to the extent of sharing the experience with us.* Rather than unanswered prayer for healing pushing us away from God, it should cause us to draw near—and nearer still.

God Is Sovereign

When we question God's actions or doubt his faithfulness, we are finite creatures with finite minds trying to understand an infinite God. In many ways we have created God in our own image, expecting him to behave as we would, judging him by our standards, forcing upon him our definitions of goodness, justice, and fairness. It is a tough lesson to learn that humans need a system of justice, but God does not. God sets the standards of human behavior, but he himself is not bound to them unless he chooses to be.

From our earliest beginnings as Christians we are taught, sometimes falsely, how God acts—we begin to feel we have God figured out. As one pastor said to me recently, "I've got all the God stuff figured out." Chilling words. But God often colors outside the lines we have drawn for him. Two suggestions might be helpful here:

First, God Works on a Different Schedule Than We Do

We are time-space creatures; everything that happens to us happens in time and space. Painfully aware of our limited time and that this time is passing rapidly, we keep calendars, wear watches, and fix schedules. For us there is past, present, and future. For God there is only the present, the eternal now.

God invariably takes longer than we expect, as he did with Abraham and Sarah, as he did with Moses, as he almost always does. He takes the long look, for with him a thousand years are as a day and a day is as a thousand years (I can identify with that last one). This present life makes sense only in the light of eternity. With God, timing is more important than time.

Second, God Works with a Different Value System

For us the words *good* and *blessing* signify comfort and convenience and happy circumstances. But to God the same words may signify character and virtue and integrity. We think in physical and material terms; God thinks in spiritual terms. To him, holiness is better than happiness, character more desirable than comfort.

We wear gold rings and gold watches; we pay much for them and more to insure them. In heaven they use gold for asphalt. What we wear down here, they walk on up there. I'm confident that if I should appear in heaven with my gold ring, the Angel of Maintenance would say, "Good, we have a few potholes that need filling."

If we fully understood the ways of God, doubt would never hound our faith. Shirley Guthrie says, "To live by faith in that *kind* of sovereign God means to expect and experience the presence and work of God in our own lives and in the world around us when there are pain and sorrow, suffering and dying, as well as when there are health, happiness, and success; when there are tragic as well as happy endings . . . Because He is so powerful that nothing can happen to us so painful that God cannot be with us and for us in the midst of it."[5]

If God Says No, Remember . . .

There is evil in the world. This is a fallen world, even for Christians. Everything wrong in the earth is man's fault; it is not as God originally created it. Further, God has not promised us an exemption from suffering. The Bible abounds with examples of the best men and women suffering through no fault of their own, especially Christ. And we cannot expect the grace of God to do for us what it did not do for Christ—exempt him from evil, suffering, and death.

God is omnipotent but he honors man's freedom. Freedom is mankind's greatest blessing and also our greatest curse. We have freedom to choose but must suffer the consequences of wrong choices. And the history of the human race is a story of bad choices. It is interesting how willing we are to take away the freedom of people like Hitler and Stalin so they cannot do the awful things they did. But if God removes one person's freedom, he must remove it from us all. None of us wants freedom taken away.

Freedom does not mean control. We may exercise our freedom to choose with the best wisdom possible, but in the end we cannot control the circumstances of life. The only thing we can control is our *reaction* to the things we cannot control.

God intervenes to further his redemptive purpose in the earth. "Tied to redemption" was the phrase used by earlier conservative theologians. Everything God does, he does to further his redemptive purpose. Prayer in "Jesus' name" is more than a formula, meaning that we pray in accord with the revelation of God's character and purpose manifest in Jesus Christ. He answers prayer and performs miracles that will cause us and others to glorify and honor him.

Embrace the suffering God and his will. God chooses to be present in the finitude and frailty of this people. He enters into our suffering and experiences our life, not just so he can experience it, but so that he can work creatively within it. Mark's account of Jesus' prayer in Gethsemane and his subsequent crucifixion (see Mark 14–15) brings together the theme of divine power and the necessity of suffering.

Sharyn Echols Dowd says, "The reconciliation of these two competing emphases takes place in a prayer scene. Prayer, which previously in the narrative has been associated with the accessibility of power, now becomes the activity in which suffering is faced and accepted . . . What . . . Jesus finally chose in prayer is not power or suffering, but the will of God. Jesus is the one character in the gospel who does the will of God when it involves participating in the divine power and also when it involves suffering and death . . . What makes both power and suffering redemptive is their character as 'will of God' . . . [His followers are] influenced to prayer, expecting power and accepting suffering."[6]

Give voice to your pain. By this I don't mean talking about the disease, diagnosis, and doctors, but rather your *feelings* and your *fears* concerning your illness. Too many sick persons are deprived of conversation. When we try to express our "illness," we simply can't say how we feel—as Christians we believe we must put it into acceptable spiritualese, which is always inadequate. Our feelings of fear and dread must be "a lack of faith," and therefore, sin, which only adds guilt to everything else we're feeling.

Illness takes away parts of your life, and these losses must be mourned, must be talked about, shared. Arthur Frank says, "Ill persons have a great deal to say for themselves, but rarely do I hear them talk about their hopes and fears, about what it feels like to be in pain, about what sense they make of suffering and the prospect of death. Because such talk embarrasses us, we do not have practice with it."[7]

To elevate our illness beyond mere pain and loss, we must learn to talk about it, and others must learn to listen with compassion, not judgment.

God was a Savior before he was a Creator. I have great news for all sufferers. In our thinking we usually place creation as the first revealed act of God, but the Bible makes clear that he was Redeemer before Creator:

For He was foreknown before the foundation of
the world, but has appeared in these last times.
(1 Pet. 1:20)

Just as He chose us in Him before the foundation of the world. (Eph. 1:4)

And we know that God causes all things to
work together for good to those who love God, to
those who are called according to His purpose. For
those whom He foreknew, He also predestined to
become conformed to the image of His Son, so that
He would be the firstborn among many brethren.
(Rom. 8:28–29)

Jesus was the Lamb slain for our sin before the foundation
of the world. Before there was a garden of Eden, there was a hill
called Calvary; before there was a Tree of Life, there was the cross
of Christ; before there was sin, there was a Savior. This should
say to us that whatever happens to us in this world, we can never
question his love—even when he says no.

I close this chapter with words found on a plaque in a reha-
bilitation hospital. The origin of these words is uncertain; they
are believed to have been penned by a Civil War soldier who had
endured more than his share of personal suffering.

A Creed for Those Who Have Suffered

I asked God for strength, that I might achieve.
I was made weak, that I might learn humbly to
    obey . . .

I asked for health, that I might do great things.
I was given infirmity, that I might do better
   things . . .
I asked for power, that I might have the praise of
   men.
I was given weakness, that I might feel the need of
   God . . .
I asked for all things, that I might enjoy life.
I was given life, that I might enjoy all things . . .
I got nothing I asked for—but everything that I had
   hoped for.
Almost despite myself, my unspoken prayers were
   answered.
I am, among men, most richly blessed!

CHAPTER 18

"I've Come to Help You Die"

There Are No Cures, Only Postponements

IN A SMALL TOWN IN England a young mother lay dying of cancer. She believed God wanted to heal her. Every day people from her church gathered around her bed, praying for her healing, claiming her healing, urging her to claim her healing. "You are healed," they'd say to her. She agreed.

One day a pastor who knew the young family ran into her husband. "How is your wife doing?" he asked. The husband dropped his head and said, "She's much worse. Two weeks ago, she began to deteriorate rapidly."

The pastor asked, "Are her friends still coming by to pray for her?"

"No. They haven't been around in two weeks."

"Would it be all right if I came to see her?" the pastor asked.

"Would you please?"

The next day the pastor quietly entered the bedroom and was shocked to see the change since his last visit. Her body was shrunken, her face pale and sunken. The familiar smell of death smothered the room. The pastor, thinking she was asleep, tiptoed to the bed. Suddenly her eyes opened and saw the pastor.

"Oh, Pastor," she whispered, "have you come to pray for my healing?"

The pastor gently sat down on the edge of the bed and, taking her hand in his, said, "No, Doris. I haven't come to pray for your healing. I've come to help you die."

Tears filled her eyes.

"Oh Pastor," she cried, "thank you! Thank you!"

And for the next hour the pastor read Scripture after Scripture to her, assuring her of God's presence, pointing her to the glory that awaited her.

As the pastor told me the story, one beautiful phrase kept repeating itself in my mind: "I've come to help you die."

The Last Thing We Talk About

There are no cures, only postponements. We live continually in the shadow of death, so real, so inevitable—yet we don't like to talk about it. As one young woman said, "Dying just scares me to death." And we are encouraged in our silence by a society that reveres youth and despises old age, that hides the old and sick in institutions, that seeks to conceal the fact of death by any means possible.

We don't even use the right words. We say they have "passed away" or "passed on." Elisabeth Kubler-Ross tells of the time she approached the head of a six-hundred-bed facility and said, "I'd like to work with some dying people." The administrator said, "In our hospital, nobody dies. They expire."[1] The taboo that the Victorians placed on public discussion of sex has now been transferred to a public discussion of death in our society. Joseph Bayly wrote that "the combination of cultural death-denial and absence of opportunity to observe the death event produces heightened fear of death in many people."[2]

I believe we should never give up hope for healing nor take that hope away from the patient. We should keep praying for healing as long as God gives us peace to do so. But when it becomes obvious that the illness is going to terminate in death, we have a further, and I believe greater, duty to help that person die in dignity and peace.

To Tell or Not to Tell

To tell or not to tell, that is the question.

As far back as I can remember, the answer to that question was almost always no. Most often even the loved ones of the dying person did not want to know. It seemed that to accept the fact was to accept defeat, to admit that somehow our faith had failed. So we pretended to ourselves and to others that death was not a reality in this case. Of course, everyone *knew* the patient was dying, and eventually the patient himself became aware of it. As Rabbi Earl Grollman, in his book *Coping with Death and Dying*, writes,

> They sense it by the changed attention, by the new and different approach that people take to them, by the lowering of voices or avoidance of sounds, by the tearful face of a relative or an ominous, unsmiling member of the family who cannot hide his true feeling.[3]

And so the absurd dance begins. We know she is dying, she knows she is dying, she knows that we know she's dying, we know that she knows we know, and we all pretend nobody knows. I'm not so sure but that our refusal to tell is to protect our own feelings as much as the patient's. By not telling her what she suspects or already knows, we do her a disservice and deprive ourselves and her of the opportunity of ministry.

In 1972 my mother was diagnosed with colon cancer. By 1973 it had moved to the liver and she knew she was going to die. In October of that year she and Dad came from Arkansas to visit us in Dallas. One day when Mom and I were alone, she said, "Nobody talks about it. Everyone tiptoes around the subject, as though I'm not sick. I need to talk about it." She was a victim of the "Third Person Syndrome," her real needs ignored, a casualty of pretense. Of course, I was quiet about the subject because I was afraid of causing her pain. But what she needed and wanted was honesty, not sugarcoated conversation. And so we talked.

She died the next year. Not long after that I noticed a piece of paper tucked between two books in my bookcase. I pulled it out and read it. It was a short note in Mom's handwriting: "I love you Ronald Louis Dunn. October 24, 1973." I think she was trying to tell me thanks for letting her talk.

Sherwin B. Nuland, in his book *How We Die*, tells that when his aunt Rose was dying of aggressive lymphoma, he and other members of the family persuaded the doctor not to tell her of her condition. Later, he writes,

> Without perhaps even realizing it, we had committed one of the worst errors that can be made in a terminal illness—all of us, Rose included, had decided incorrectly and in opposition to every principle of our lives together that it was more important to protect one another from the open admission of a painful truth than it was to achieve a final sharing that might have snatched an enduring

comfort and even some dignity from the anguish-
ing fact of death. We denied ourselves what should
have been ours.[4]

I especially appreciate the conclusion Dr. Nulan draws from
this experience:

> A promise we can keep and a hope we can give
> is the certainty that no man or woman will be left to
> die alone. Of the many ways to die alone, the most
> comfortless and solitary must surely take place
> when the knowledge of death's certainty is withheld.
> Here again, it is the "I couldn't take away his hope"
> attitude that is so often precisely how a particularly
> reassuring form of hope is never allowed to materi-
> alize. Unless we are aware that we are dying and as
> far as possible know the conditions of our death, we
> cannot share any sort of final consummation with
> those who love us. Without this consummation,
> no matter their presence at the hour of passing, we
> will remain unattended and isolated. For it is the
> promise of spiritual companionship near the end
> that gives us hope, much more than does the mere
> offsetting of the fear of being physically without
> anyone.[5]

Though there may be situations where it might be best not to
tell, it seems to me that a dying person has the right, and the need,
to know that he is dying.

First, acknowledging the fact may relieve the patient of the
burden of pretending, a relief to stop being strong for everyone
else, to cease behaving according to others' expectations. Doris,
whose story we told at the beginning of this chapter, found a great

burden lifted when she was able to acknowledge the fact that she was dying. We add an extra load onto the patient when we expect him to keep up the pretense.

Second, a dying person may need to set things in order—legal affairs, spiritual matters, a thousand things. Knowing he is dying, a person may need to make amends with certain people. The dying patient needs to be able to do this while he or she still has the strength and mental capacity to deal with such matters.

Third, knowing the truth gives all concerned a chance to say good-bye. I have talked to many mourners whose great regret was, "I never got to say good-bye." Some of these have traveled to the cemetery alone to say their good-byes in privacy. Other have written letters to the deceased person as a form of farewell. Being able to say good-bye helps bring about a closure and definitely aids in the grief process to follow

The dying person has the right to say good-bye to his family and friends. I have already told Kaye that I want to be told. If I knew I was dying there are some things I would want to say to my wife and children. If my wife were dying, there are some things I would want to say to her.

One mourner I talked to was a member of a family who believed strongly in atonement healing. Before entering her father's hospital room, she was always cautioned never to say anything negative, for it might upset the balance of faith. She was never allowed to be honest with her father, never able to tell him good-bye and what he had meant to her. She was afraid that if she were honest and told her dad good-bye, then she might be accused of breaking the chain of faith, resulting in her father's death. I have talked to many in this situation and, to me, it is one of the crueler aspects of atonement-healing doctrine.

When my dad lay dying of cancer in the hospital, I faced this dilemma. I knew he was dying, and I was pretty sure that he knew, although nothing had been said. But I wasn't going to let my father go without telling him some things. One day I found myself in the room alone with him. His eyes were closed, but I knew he wasn't asleep. Already plans were underway to move him to the hospice wing of the hospital. I knew I couldn't wait any longer. Taking his hand, I leaned over and whispered in this ear. I didn't tell him he was dying. I told him how proud I was of him—he never finished high school but worked six days a week, sunup to sundown, and became a more than successful businessman. I was proud of that, I told him. I was proud to be his son and thanked him for the home he provided for us and for giving us a Christian upbringing. I said many things, Dad never said a word, but when I finished speaking, he opened his eyes and looked at me. His eyes were filled with tears, and I knew he was grateful to hear the things I said. That was some time ago, and to this day it remains one of my most precious memories concerning my dad.

"I've Come to Help You Die"

Most of us feel a great sense of inadequacy when illness or tragedy hits someone we know. I talk to many survivors who are mystified and hurt because friends won't talk to them about their situation. Sometimes this may be due to thoughtlessness and insensitivity, but most of the time it is the result of feelings of powerlessness and fear of saying the wrong thing.

I always considered myself a loner, thinking I would not need people if tragedy ever struck. But when tragedy did strike, I discovered an insatiable thirst for people—people who knew what had happened and cared and were willing for the world to stop because of it.

Having ministered to many families facing this situation, having learned from both my helpful moments and from my mistakes, and having said tearful farewells to loved ones of my own, I have some suggestions for helping a friend or loved one die.

Assure them that they are not alone. We are there and will be there for them. In his fascinating story *The Death of Ivan Ilyich*, Tolstoy tells the story of a man who faced the terrible solitude of a death made lonely by withholding the truth. "This solitude through which he was passing, as he lay with his face turned to the back of the divan—a solitude amid a populous city, and amid his numerous circle of friends and family—a solitude deeper than which could not be found anywhere, either in the depths of the sea, or in the earth . . . and he had to live thus on the edge of destruction—alone, without anyone to understand and pity him."

Sadly, the tendency today is to isolate the dying patients in hospitals, behind drawn curtains, with threatening signs: "No Visitors." But no one should die alone. If the person is dying, your presence can't make him worse. You don't need to say anything; just holding his hand says, "You are not alone. You are not forgotten."

Encourage them to talk through their feelings and fears. "We need to realize that the believer can maintain a steadfast hope in God and still experience great turmoil in the face of death."[6] Helping dying friends to open up and talk about their illness is one of the greatest gifts you can give. It isn't a lack of faith for patients to express their fears of dying, of what might happen to those left behind. They may have a desperate need to share these feelings but fear doing so will cause others to doubt their trust in the Lord. It is our duty to allow them to say such things without fear of judgment.

Listen. People often tell me, "I don't know what to say." Saying something is not the important thing. Being there with a listening ear is. If they want to talk about their death, don't interrupt with statements like, "Oh, don't even mention that. You're not going to die." Let the sick person set the agenda. They may ramble, but fix your eyes on theirs and concentrate on what they are saying. Betsy Burnham, who died of cancer in 1982, wrote, "Listening is one of the first, best steps in helping your friend win the emotional, mental and spiritual battles that accompany illness. A listening friend faces your inner struggles with you, bearing the burden at your side, leaving you with more energy to fight the battle for life."[7]

Relive the happy moments of their life. "Remember when you and I went . . ." may be just the words that will help the patient appreciate the life he has lived.

Most of all, assure them of God's continuing presence. Remind them of God's promises to those who are suffering. Promises like Hebrews 13:5, where Christ promises never to leave us or forsake us, and Romans 8:35–39, which assures us that not even death can separate us from God's love, can give the dying person much comfort. Being a Christian doesn't mean that we don't die, but our death is different—we see death as a *defeated* enemy. The fact that death cannot threaten our relationship to God is the key to a Christian approach to death and dying.

Focus on the glories that are to come. For Christians who die, it is not just a matter of saying good-bye to us but also of saying hello to the Lord Jesus and to our loved ones who have gone before. Read to them John's description of what the Christian's home-going will be like in Revelation 21:1–5.

Max Lucado closes his book *The Applause of Heaven* with these special words to all who have embraced Jesus Christ as Savior and Lord: "Before you know it, your appointed arrival time will come; you'll descend the ramp and enter the City. You'll see faces that are waiting for you. You'll hear your name spoken by those who love you. And maybe, just maybe—in the back, behind the crowds—the One who would rather die than live without you will remove his pierced hands from his heavenly robe and . . . *applaud.*"[8]

There is more to death than the dying—there is the promise of a waiting Savior. Why not celebrate that while the person is facing death?

CHAPTER 19

Something Better than Healing

The "God-Ultimate Purpose" of Suffering

LET ME INTRODUCE YOU TO a man who taught me more about suffering than anyone I've ever known.

To those of us who knew him, the only thing surprising about Manley Beasley's death was that he actually died. I told him once that he was a hard man to say good-bye to. On at least four occasions Kaye and I, being informed that Manley wouldn't make it through the day, visited the hospital to say good-bye. We were thwarted every time. Again and again God raised him from his deathbed and gave him a greater ministry.

Manley was tall, handsome, and a revivalist in the grand tradition. In 1997 he fell ill to Collangen Vascular Disease, a disease that spawns scleroderma, lupus, dermatomyositis, and polymyositis. These are generally considered fatal diseases. At the same time, he was afflicted with four other lesser diseases. At first he wasn't given much more than a year to live—he was, for all practical purposes, an invalid.

He lived in great pain, greater than most people could imagine. Yet I never heard him once complain about his pain or his illnesses. During this time God gave him a promise that he would "live to see his children's children." I told Manley that if God gave me that promise, I would never let any of my children marry.

Manley was my best friend. He taught me more about faith and walking with God than anyone I have ever known. About a year before he died, we sat down together, and Manley allowed me to talk to him about his illnesses, sufferings, and the place of God in it all.

DUNN: One of the first times I heard you speak, you had just come from a lengthy stay in the hospital, and your first words were, "Folks, God won't hurt you." To me it sure looked like God was hurting you. At the time I thought he was killing you. What did you mean by that statement?

BEASLEY: I think it's like a woman bearing a child—there's a great deal of pain in that. But after she holds that baby in her arms, she forgets the pain. At the time of whatever suffering you're going through, it does seem as though God is hurting, even killing you. But when you've gone through it and look back upon the benefits of it, you forget the pain. As I look back upon my suffering, I see that it was all very good. That "very good" attitude comes from turning that adversity over to God and allowing him to teach me his purpose in it.

DUNN: The reason I ask is that most of us in the midst of suffering feel such desolation and despair that we wonder if God is anywhere around.

BEASLEY: That's absolutely true. But there are some facts you can know about God even in the midst of the struggle. I know that God is in charge and that he is aware of the situation and that he is allowing this for his glory and also limiting it according to his will. These things you can know even though you are in pain—that does not, however, necessarily keep you from despairing. During my last hospitalization, there were times when I hurt so bad I would cry. I was in a dilemma at times as to what was going on, but I knew God was there. That was comfort in the midst of battle.

DUNN: In other words, there is a deeper issue involved in this beyond whether you are healed or whether you die.

BEASLEY: Yes. That is one of the unique points about any suffering—there is a God-ultimate purpose. That God-ultimate purpose is to correct us and enlarge us and bring us through for his glory. Paul said that whether he lived or died, he wanted God to be glorified. Paul had gotten to the ultimate purpose of God. The suffering in itself is just a vehicle by which God moves us up as he moved Job up. Job was saying, "I have heard you with my ears, but now since I've gone through all this, I see you with my spiritual eyes." God, through suffering, enlarged Job's capacity to know God. He went from the hearing of the ear to the seeing of the eye.

DUNN: You first began having serious health problems in 1970. Since then those have been compounded by other difficulties, but you said that this last year was your worst. It's easy to have certain opinions about pain and suffering if we've never experienced any. But after being put in that crucible, sometimes our beliefs change and we pray differently. Has your praying changed from 1970 until now?

BEASLEY: I pray differently now because I know what God is up to. The first time I was asking God, "What's going on?" Now I do not ask that. I simply say, "Lord, I know you are doing a work and I want to cooperate with you." So I did change somewhat, but not my views about God and healing. I just react differently. I struggled with death the first time; now I struggle with death physically, but I do not struggle in my spirit with death. You have to realize most people never face death until they die. I have faced it every day for almost twenty years. I am supposed to be dead, ought to be dead—and if it was not for the sustaining life of God—I would be dead today.

DUNN: Obviously what we are both saying is that the greater issue is the glory of God. Do you think God is more glorified by not healing you than he would have been had he instantly and totally healed you?

BEASLEY: That's a good question. One day I sensed the Lord saying to me, "I can heal you if you want me to, or I can leave you like you are. To leave you like you are, you will have to have me every day to keep you going." I made a deliberate choice to trust the Lord every day because I felt that if God healed me instantly, it would become something in my past that would grow dimmer in my memory. Whereas, if I had to have him every day he would remain fresh and real to me. I've seen many people have a miraculous healing and ten years down the road they were just as full of the Devil as they ever were. But with me, twenty years down the road, I am still having to trust God every day to keep me alive.

DUNN: In other words, you don't just preach sermons, you are the sermon. Like Jeremiah, you don't just give a proclamation, you are that proclamation.

BEASLEY: I have had to come to the fact that my life is the message as much as my verbalizing the message. Many times when I step into the pulpit, people will give me a standing ovation. Initially I wanted to rebuke them for doing that, but the Lord rebuked me and said, "Son, they are not clapping for you; they are clapping for what I am doing in your life. Leave them alone."

DUNN: This brings up a most important question: Must God take us through some suffering, some brokenness, if we are to be what he wants us to be?

BEASLEY: I think it is possible for a person to get through life successfully without going through a breaking, but I don't think it's probable. Most of the people in the Bible that God used mightily went through a breaking of some sort, and the great Christians I have studied all experienced something similar. It would be foolish of me to say that all suffering must be physical, for often the emotional trauma is worse than the physical.

What happens is that you get to wanting God so much, to be so real to yourself and others, that you are willing to pay any price.

DUNN: When you were released from the hospital last November, I called you, and you told me something that intrigued me. You said, "God has said a lot of things to me, but I don't think people want to hear them." What did you mean by that? And what are people looking for from you? Are they hoping for a simple answer?

BEASLEY: Ron, this is possibly the most difficult thing for me to communicate. I am still putting together all the things the Lord showed me. You know, you can know things in your spirit that you don't understand in your mind. Only when you come to understand in your mind what you know in the spirit can you communicate it to people.

They tell me that I literally died six times—that my heart quit beating and I stopped breathing. Six times. I wondered why God did not show me heaven, as we hear he did from others who "died." I asked him why, and he showed me that if I had seen heaven, I would not have wanted to come back. Paul saw enough that he said he wasn't sure whether he wanted to stay here or go on to be with the Lord.

People want healing or an explanation—they are looking for a quick formula that they can take like an aspirin and in a matter of minutes it will all be over. But that way would totally defeat the purpose of God in allowing the suffering. The suffering prepares us for the revelation God has for us of himself in our lives.

Recently a young man who was about to have a brain tumor removed called and asked me to pray for him. The operation was not fully successful. He was given six weeks to six months to live. The man, an outstanding revivalist, asked to talk to me. "What do you do," he asked, "when they tell you that you have, at the most, six months to live?"

I said to him, "Well, you do what you should do and that is simply trust Jesus with your life."

"I don't understand," he said.

"Well, my family was called in six times and told that I wouldn't last till noon, and that is what we did—just trusted Jesus with my life."

That's what people don't want to hear.

DUNN: You're saying, I think, that if we believe all our suffering is the Devil's doing, then our primary, possibly our only, motive is to get rid of it. But if we see God in it, that makes a difference. Our primary motive is not to get rid of suffering but to find what God is trying to say to us.

BEASLEY: Exactly. A woman with a terminal illness came to see me. She and her husband were missionaries. When I met her, the first thing the Lord impressed me to do was ask her why she was ill. I knew she was going to think that was a stupid question, but I obeyed the Lord.

RON DUNN

"Why do you think you are ill?" I said.

"I don't know," she answered.

I said, "If you knew why you are ill, you might not want to get rid of it."

DUNN: When I called you in November, you said the turning point came when you were able to get hold of God. Talk about that.

BEASLEY: There was a time in two unique crises—I'm referring to the first time I was hospitalized in Houston for four months, then again in 1988, when I was in the hospital five and a half months—in both cases it looked like God had literally forsaken me. I think there were two reasons for that. One, there are times when God withdraws his conscious presence from us to teach us to walk alone in obedience without the crutch of his conscious presence. The other reason we are unconscious of God in times of struggle is because our spirit is like the sea. If the sea is calm, you can drop a hair on it and it will make a ripple. But if the spirit is disturbed, when the sea is raging, you could drop a mountain into it and no one would take notice.

So God must get you to a place where there is quietness, stillness, and calmness before he can really talk to you. Then when he does, when you get to God, the victory is there. Even though the suffering may intensify, the victory is there. Often when people think God has abandoned them, he has just backed up to give them an opportunity to realize where they are and what they will do in circumstances like that.

DUNN: So you're saying that the deepest part of pain is not so much the physical suffering but the sense of being cut off from God?

BEASLEY: Yes. I believe Christ's greatest suffering on the cross was when he cried out, "My God, why hast thou forsaken me?"

DUNN: I think that is so important for people to hear because most of us look at your life and assume that you never had a point of desperation when you felt abandoned by God. We look at you and say, "I wish I had Manley Beasley's faith." I remember after that phone call—I never felt the Spirit of God so strong through a phone line—Kaye and I talked about it for a while. I said, "I'm glad I've never had to go through what Manley's gone through." Immediately, the Lord rebuked me: "Why don't you just go ahead and say it, 'I'm glad that I'm not as close to God as Manley is.'" We all want your faith, but we don't want to go to the school where you learned it.

BEASLEY: Well, one of the real issues is ministry, making it possible for the glory of God to be revealed through you. At first I used to fuss at God about my condition. But I stopped fussing at God and surrendered to his purpose. As a result, I am speaking to more people, seeing more people saved, seeing more of God's glory than I ever did when I was in perfect health. That is fascinating to me.

DUNN: If suddenly I find myself terribly ill and the doctors say that I have six weeks to six months to live, how do I pray? What do I say?

BEASLEY: I would naturally cry out to God. For a Christian, this should always be their first response: Cry out to God. Ask God for healing, but much more, ask him to get you to the place where you can say, "Lord, be glorified in my life." It might take some time. It took me seven months to get there when I first got sick. I had never been ill—I was thirty-nine years old and going strong for the Lord. It didn't make sense—at first.

But to get back to your question: I would pray, "Lord, help me make the corrections and see the purpose in this so I can enjoy your presence even in pain." That's what I would do.

DUNN: Well, Manley, I have one last question: Was it worth it?

BEASLEY: Ron, if I had a thousand lives and knew that all of them would be like this one, I would give them all to him because I think it is worth it. To have the joy and peace that you are prepared for whatever life throws at you—that is great assurance, and it is a very comforting position to be in. I rejoice in being in that position, and so I thank God. I count it all joy.

Manley Beasley died in July of 1990.

I am convinced, as was Manley, that he could have been healed had he chosen to be. God promised him that. Tough choice. But, considering his life, ministry, and influence, I believe he made the right choice.

CHAPTER 20

Fear Not

We Can Have Joy in the Presence of Heartache

AN ANCIENT LEGEND TELLS OF a man traveling in his carriage to Constantinople. Suddenly in the middle of the road an old man appears, wearing a heavy cloak and hood, his arms stretched high to the heavens. The traveler brings his carriage to an abrupt halt, and the strange figure appears at the traveler's side. His eyes burning, he says, "Take me to Constantinople!"

"Who are you?" the traveler demands.

The hooded figure says, "My name is Cholera. Take me to Constantinople!"

The traveler draws back in terror, "No!" he shouts with a trembling voice. "You will kill the city!"

"I could kill you now," Cholera whispers. "But take me to Constantinople, and I promise I will kill only five people."

Reluctantly, the traveler bids the old man to get into the carriage and delivers him to Constantinople.

Two weeks later 120 people have died in the city. Meeting Cholera on the street one day, the traveler accosts him and shrieks, "You lied! You said you would kill only five people."

Cholera shakes himself loose from the traveler's grip. "I didn't lie. I kept my promise. I killed only five. *Fear killed the rest.*"

Fear killed the rest! Where disease kills its hundreds, fear kills its thousands. Biologists tell us that fear is one of the first and strongest emotions developed in humans and animals. Fear and anxiety haunt people from the cradle to the grave, betraying their spirit, breaking down their defenses, and making them unfit for the work of living.

Nowhere does this emotion express itself more forcefully than when we are confronted with sickness, suffering, and death—not just the fear of dying, but the fear of the illness itself, of what it will do to our lives, of living with chronic pain or disability. The strongest Christian is not immune to this initial reaction.

But I believe there is an answer to this fear, a cure for the anxiety borne by the one facing suffering. The words of Jesus to John on the Isle of Patmos have helped me through many a scary situation. When John beheld the risen and glorified Lord in all his glory, he said, "When I saw Him, I fell at His feet like a dead man. And He placed His right hand upon me, saying, 'Do not be afraid; I am the first and the last, and the living One; and I was dead, and behold, I am alive forevermore, and I have the keys of death and of Hades'" (Rev. 1:17–18).

"Fear not" is one of the most frequent greetings of Christ to his people. When the angel brought his message to Mary, he said, "Fear not." When Jesus called Peter to follow him, he said, "Fear not." When speaking of the enemies that would persecute his followers, he said, "Fear not." Concerning the everyday needs of his disciples, he said, "Fear not." When speaking of sickness and death in Luke 8:50 (KJV), he said, "Fear not."

Don't Be Afraid of Life

To many people there are some things worse than dying—and living is one of them. Seventeen people a day in the United States prove it by committing suicide. Many are more afraid of life than death. To them Jesus says, "Do not be afraid; I am the first and the last, and the Living One . . . I am alive forevermore" (Rev. 1:17–18).

To quell John's fear Jesus laid his right hand upon the beloved apostle. The right hand, the hand of favor and power that supports the weak, lifts up the fallen, and gives strength to those who have no strength. When Christ ministered to the needy, he put his right hand upon them—the blind, the deaf, even the leper. And that gesture was always half the cure.

John had felt that right hand many times before. That touch let him know that Christ was still there, still the same. Although Jesus' hand changed in his outward glory, in his nature and heart and compassion, he was still the same.

"I am the first and the last," Jesus said. He is present at the beginning and at the end. He is there at the moment of birth and the moment of death. He is there when we set out on our Christian journey, and he is there when we finish our course.

When the kings of the earth sleep in the dust of the ground and their power has vanished like a wisp of smoke, when all the enduring monuments of the world have turned into the mists that the morning sun drives away, when all the great people of the earth lie silent in their graves, Jesus will still be here.

It was the *known* presence of Jesus that calmed the apostle's heart. Christ does not say to us, "Fear not, here is a million dollars," or, "Fear not, here is a miracle drug." He says, "Fear not, it is I." Jesus' presence always banished fear, and it still does. Our greatest asset during times of suffering is the presence of Jesus.

Jesus said, "I will never desert you, nor will I ever forsake you" (Heb. 13:5).

The one constant in the believer's life is the presence of Jesus. Teilhard de Chardin was right when he said, "Joy is not the absence of pain but the presence of God."

Don't Be Afraid of Death

Christ has changed death. Although death is an enemy, "the last enemy that will be abolished" (1 Cor. 15:26), it is also a friend. To the Corinthians Paul said, "Therefore, being always of good courage, and knowing that while we are at home in the body we are absent from the Lord—for we walk by faith not by sight—we are of good courage, I say, and prefer rather to be absent from the body and to be at home with the Lord" (2 Cor. 5:6–8). The same thought was expressed in his letter to the Philippians: "But I am hard-pressed from both directions, having the desire to depart and be with Christ, for that is very much better" (Phil. 1:23).

Death for the believer is no longer just death. It is sleep. When we die, we fall asleep in Jesus, laying aside this house of clay for a little while. Death means going to be with Jesus—which is far better. Like sleep, death for us is temporary and has its awakening.

Christ controls death. "I have the keys of death and Hades." Think of it. The Devil doesn't have the keys to his own house! The keys are a symbol of authority, of control, of possession and government. As terrible as it is, death is not allowed to run rampant without control. Nothing happens by chance. All history lies in the elective purpose of God. Even death is in the hands of God. It moves only at the permissive will of heaven.

Christ holds the key to the door of death, and no one enters it unless our Christ uses the key and opens it.

Christ conquered death. "I was dead, and behold, I am alive forevermore." Death for the Christian isn't permanent or final. Death will not hold our bodies forever. Christ died and survived the grave, and because he lives we shall live also. Christ shares his victory with us.

Julian, the Apostate, was the nephew of the Roman Caesar Constantine and was reared in a Christian family. But in his youth he renounced his faith and embraced paganism. When he became emperor in AD 361, he tried to blot out Christianity. While leading a humble Christian to his death, one of Julian's followers mocked, "And where is your carpenter God now?" The Christian replied, "He's building a coffin for your emperor."

And he was, for in AD 363 Julian, facing a Persian army, died on the battlefield. One of the most famous incidents in history is that as they carried the dying emperor off the field of battle, he lifted his eyes to heaven and said, "Oh, pale Galilean, thou hast conquered."

Don't Be Afraid of Eternity

"I fell at His feet like a dead man." Doesn't the reaction of John strike you as strange? Instead of ecstatic joy and bliss at seeing Jesus, he is filled with fear. Why?

John could look undaunted at the throne of jasper, the emerald rainbow, the seven lamps burning before the throne of God, the crystal seas, and the doors of heaven. You would think that after nearly sixty years John would be rejoicing at the sight of his Lord.

But now John is looking at unveiled deity, the Ancient of Days, whose countenance shines like the sun. He is looking into the eyes of the judge of all the earth, eyes that burn like fire—and he falls at Jesus' feet as a dead man.

This exemplifies the fear of meeting face-to-face the exalted judge of all the earth. In Revelation 6, the fear is so great that people call for the mountains and rocks to fall on them to hide them from his face. He is the judge on the throne "from whose face heaven and earth fled away." Heaven and earth have been mute witnesses to Satan's rebellion in heaven, the lighting of the fires of hell, the chaining of fallen angels, the flood, the destruction of Sodom, the famine in Jerusalem where mothers ate their own babies. They have seen it all. But at the sight of the eternal judge, they flee in terror.

But Jesus says, "Do not be afraid . . . I have the keys of Hades." Hades and hell (*ghenna*) are not the same. Hades is the unseen world, the world of men's souls and heavenly spirits, the world on the other side of the grave—eternity. "Keys" is plural, conveying the idea that double power is referred to, the power to keep from hell or to consign to hell. Whether souls are damned and in hell or glorified and in heaven, Christ is Lord of all.

The unseen world is a good name for it, for we fear what we cannot see, what we do not know, but from that unseen world, Jesus says, "Fear not." Don't be afraid of eternity. Don't be afraid of what lies on the other side of the grave.

When I was ten years old, our Cub Scout den went on an excursion, the purpose of which was to teach us to read a compass. There were four groups of four cub Scouts with a Boy Scout assigned to lead each group. Our den leaders drove us up to the Boston Mountains near Fort Smith, Arkansas, and let us out at different spots. It was ten o'clock at night. It had been raining all day, and the clouds obscured what little moonlight there was. We were given our compass reading and headed out. The compass reading would take us to a lodge where hot chocolate and Oreo cookies would be waiting.

Unfortunately, this was before the bunny batteries, and before long our flashlight shone dim, dimmer, and finally dark. Without any light at all, we could barely see the compass, much less read it. Our hike to the lodge was to take only an hour. Two hours later we knew we were lost, tripping over dead branches and falling into wet leaves. The Boy Scout, who had done this before (done what before? Been lost?), led us in what he thought was the right direction.

Suddenly the ground in front of us was even darker than the ground we had been stumbling over. It meant one thing—we had come to a drop-off. The pitch blackness of the night kept us from knowing whether it was a drop-off of three feet or three hundred feet. We didn't move an inch, except backward. The tantalizing thing about it was that about one hundred yards forward we could see the lights of the lodge, where there was hot chocolate and Oreo cookies. They were probably being consumed even now by those who had made it on time.

We all waited for someone to do something. Somebody had to crawl down that drop-off and find out what was there. It wasn't going to be me, for sure. I was ten years old and the bravest thing I had ever done was to light a match without closing the cover. So we Cub Scouts all focused on the big, experienced Boy Scout. Finally, with a sigh of resignation, he sat down on the edge of the drop-off and dragged himself downward, giving us the unneeded exhortation not to move from that spot.

For a while we could hear him sliding down through the brush—and then nothing. Petrified, we waited. After what seemed an eternity we heard a voice from the other side of the ravine. It was our Boy Scout.

"It's okay," he called. "Come on, you can make it."

And we did. Hot chocolate and Oreo cookies never tasted so good.

Someday we will all stand on that dark edge of the unseen world. And we may be frightened. But if we listen carefully, we will hear the voice of our Leader, calling:

"It's okay. Come on, you can make it."

PART FOUR

Resources

Notes

Introduction   There's a New God in Town

1. Peter Brown, *The Body and Society* (New York: Columbia University Press, 1988), 6.

2. Lewis Thomas, *The Medusa and the Snail* (New York: Bantam Books, 1980), 37–38.

Chapter 1   When Questions Come

1. C. S. Lewis, *The Problem of Pain* (New York: Macmillan, 1962), 10.

2. Kornelis H. Miskotte, *When the Gods Are Silent* (New York: Harper and Row, 1967), 252.

Chapter 2   The Night Side of Life

1. Arthur Kleinman, *The Illness Narratives* (New York: Basic Books, 1988), 45.

2. Arthur Frank, *At the Will of the Body* (Boston: Houghton Mifflin Company, 1991), 38.

3. Thomas Bernhard, *Wittgenstein's Nephew*, trans. Edward Osers (London: Quartet Books, 1986), 56.

4. Frank, *At the Will of the Body*, 92.

5. Ibid., 20–21.

Chapter 3   Where Does Sickness Come From?

1. C. S. Lovett, *Jesus Wants You Well* (Baldwin Park, CA: *Personal Christianity*, 1973), 135.

2. Lester Packer, *Dallas Times Herald*, February 4, 1985, 2.

3. Wade H. Boggs Jr., *Faith Healing and the Christian Faith* (Richmond, VA: John Knox Press, 1956), 113.

4. M. Scott Peck, *The Road Less Traveled* (New York: Simon and Schuster, 1978), 39.

5. J. I. Packer, *Keep in Step with the Spirit* (Old Tappan, NJ: Revell, 1984), 196.

6. Boggs, *Faith Healing and the Christian Faith*, 116.

7. John W. Farquhar, *The American Way of Life Need Not Be Hazardous to Your Health* (New York: W. W. Norton and Company, 1978), vii.

8. Paul Tournier, *The Healing of Persons* (San Francisco: Harper and Row, 1979), 4–5.

9. Philip Yancey, *Where Is God When It Hurts?* (Grand Rapids: Zondervan, 1977), 73.

Chapter 4   By the Rivers of Babylon

1. Frank, *At the Will of the Body*, 91.

2. David Rabin and Pauline Rabin, *To Provide Safe Passage* (New York: Philosophical Library, 1985), 38–39, 41.

3. Max Lerner, *Wrestling with the Angel* (New York: W. W. Norton and Company, 1990), 38–39.

4. Simone Weil, quoted in Dorothee Soelle, *Suffering* (Philadelphia: Fortress Press, 1975), 114.

5. Kleinman, *Illness Narratives*, 159.

6. Howard Brody, *Stories of Sickness* (New Haven, CT: Yale University Press, 1975), 114.

7. Kleinman, *Illness Narratives*, 160.

8. Jimmy Allen, *Burden of a Secret* (Nashville: Moorings, 1995).

9. Wilfred Sheed, *In Love with Daylight* (New York: Simon and Schuster, 1995), 57.

10. Betty Sue Flowers, quoted in Kathy Cronkite, *On the Edge of Darkness* (New York: Doubleday, 1994), 204–5.

11. Kay Redfield Jamison, *An Unquiet Mind* (New York: Alfred A. Knopf, 1995), 6.

12. Ibid., 7–8.

13. Sheila Walsh, *Honestly* (Grand Rapids: Zondervan, 1996), 28.

14. Ibid., 60.

Chapter 5   The Seduction of the Sick

1. Bertrand Russell, *A History of Western Philosophy* (New York: Simon and Schuster, 1945), 3.

2. Everett Ferguson, *Backgrounds of Early Christianity* (Grand Rapids: Eerdmans, 1987), 4.

3. Wayne A. Meeks, *The Moral World of the First Christians* (Philadelphia: The Westminister Press, 1986), 19.

4. Edith Hamilton, *Mythology* (New York: New American Library, 1942), 16.

5. John Boardman, Jasper Griffin, and Oswyn Murray, eds., *The Oxford History of the Classical World* (Oxford: Oxford University Press, 1986), 13.

6. Ferguson, *Backgrounds of Early Christianity*, 5.

7. Boardman, *Oxford History*.

8. J. I. Packer, *Hot Tub Religion* (Wheaton, IL: Tyndale House, 1987), 119.

9. Ibid., 91.

10. Eric Hoffer, *The True Believer* (New York: Harper and Row, 1951), 119.

Chapter 6   The Seducers

1. Ashley Montagu and Floyd Matson, *The Dehumanization of Man* (New York: McGraw-Hill, 1983), 122.

2. Harvey Cox, *The Seduction of the Spirit* (New York: Simon and Schuster, 1973), 305.

3. Ibid., 303–5.

4. Ibid., 16.

5. Sigmund Freud, *Group Psychology and the Analysis of the Ego*, trans. and ed. James Strachey (New York: W. W. Norton and Company, 1959), 12.

6. Paul Tillich, *The Shaking of the Foundations* (New York: Charles Scribner's Sons, 1984), 91–92.

7. Freud, *Group Psychology*, 6.

8. Larry Crabb, *Inside Out* (Colorado Springs: NavPress, 1988), 14.

9. Ernest Becker, *The Denial of Death* (New York: The FreePress, 1973), 217.

10. Van B. Weigel, *Ostrich Christianity* (Lanham, MD: University Press of America, 1986), 3.

11. Becker, *The Denial of Death*, 178–79.

Chapter 7   What Do We Mean by "Healing"?

1. Ambroise Pare, "The Journey to Turin, 1537" in *Journeys in Diverse Places*, trans. Stephen Paget (New York: Collier & Son Company, 1909–1914). Also available online at www.bartleby.com/3812/1.html (accessed September 11, 2006).

2. J. Sidlow Baxter, *Divine Healing of the Body* (Grand Rapids: Zondervan, 1979), 289.

3. Andrew Weil, *Spontaneous Healing* (New York: Knopf, 1995), 6.

4. Lewis, Thomas, *The Lives of a Cell* (New York: Penguin Books, 1978), 85.

5. Boggs, *Faith Healing*, 23.

6. Baxter, *Divine Healing*, 183

Chapter 8   Handling Accurately the Word of Truth

1. Walter Bauer, ed., *A Greek-English Lexicon of the New Testament and Other Early Christian Literature,* 2nd ed., trans. William F. Arndt and F. Wilbur Gingrich (Chicago: The University of Chicago Press, 1979), 580.

2. Richard Mayhue, "Cutting It Straight," *Moody Monthly,* vol. 85, no. 1, 1984, 36.

3. Clark Pinnock, *Biblical Revelation* (Chicago: Moody Press, 1971), 208.

4. John R. Stott, *Christianity Today,* January 8, 1996

Chapter 9   Cutting It Straight: Part One

1. Catherine Marshall, *Something More* (New York: McGraw-Hill, 1974), 270.

2. Peter Donovan, *Interpreting Religious Experience* (New York: The Seabury Press, 1979), 1.

3. Packer, *Keep in Step with the Spirit,* 201.

4. Bernard Ramm, *Protestant Biblical Interpretation,* 3rd ed. (Grand Rapids: Baker, 1970), 18.

5. Ibid.

6. J. Robertson McQuilkin, *Understanding and Applying the Bible* (Chicago: Moody Press, 1983), 49.

7. Gerhard von Rad, *Old Testament Theology,* vol. 2 (New York: Harper and Row, 1965), 319–21.

8. John Bright, *The Authority of the Old Testament* (Grand Rapids: Baker, 1975), 149.

9. Warren Wiesbe, *Why Us?* (Old Tappan, NJ: Revell, 1984), 47.

10. Bernard Ramm, *Protestant Biblical Interpretation,* 1st ed. (Boston: W. A. Wilde Company, 1950), 101.

11. Wiersbe, *Why Us?* 105–6.

Chapter 10   Cutting It Straight: Part Two

1. D. A. Carson, *Exegetical Fallacies* (Grand Rapids: Baker, 1984), 106.

2. Pinnock, *Biblical Revelation,* 212–13.

3. Ramm, *Protestant Biblical Interpretation,* 107.

4. Ibid., 177–78.

5. Ibid., 105.

6. J. Sidlow Baxter, *Divine Healing of the Body* (Grand Rapids: Zondervan, 1979), 114.

7. Packer, *Keep in Step with the Spirit*, 195.

8. Dr. Phillips made this statement during a panel discussion at the 1991 Nationwide Bible Conference at the Bellevue Baptist Church in Memphis, Tennessee.

9. Baxter, *Divine Healing*, 157.

Chapter 11   Healing: The Same Yesterday, Today, and Forever?

1. Barnabas Lindars, *The Gospel of John, New Century Bible Commentary* (Grand Rapids: Eerdmans, 1972), 475.

2. J. C. Ryle, quoted in Leon Morris, *Commentary of the Gospel of John*, The New International Commentary of the New Testament (Grand Rapids: Eerdmans, 1971), 646.

3. Ibid.

4. John F. MacArthur Jr., *The Charismatics: A Doctrinal Perspective* (Grand Rapids: Zondervan, 1978), 135.

Chapter 12   The Healings of Jesus and the Apostles: A Closer Look

1. Howard Clark Kee, *Medicine, Miracle and Magic in New Testament Times* (Cambridge, England: Cambridge University Press, 1986), 1.

2. Paul Tournier, *The Healing of Persons* (San Francisco: Harper and Row, 1965), 40.

3. Claus Westermann, *Genesis 12–36: A Commentary* (Minneapolis: Augsburg, 1985), 268.

4. Paul Billheimer, *Destined to Overcome* (Minneapolis: Bethany House, 1982), 94–95.

5. Boggs, *Faith Healing*, 23.

6. Ibid., 22.

7. Hans Kung, *Eternal Life?* (New York: Doubleday, 1984), 19–20.

8. Packer, *Keep in Step with the Spirit*, 214.

9. Vance Havner, *Fourscore: Living Beyond the Promise* (Old Tappan, NJ: Revell, 1982), 18.

10. Baxter, *Divine Healing*, 123.

Chapter 13   Did Christ Die to Make Us Healthy?

1. Leon Morris, *Basic Christian Doctrines*, ed. Carl H. F. Henry (Grand Rapids: Baker. 1971), 152.

2. Margaret Clarkson, *Destined for Glory* (Grand Rapids: Eerdmans, 1983), 95.

3. Boggs, *Faith Healing*, 85.

4. Leslie D. Weatherhead, *Why Do Men Suffer?* (New York: Abingdon Press, 1936), 171.

5. C. R. Brown, *Faith and Health* (New York: Thomas Y. Cromwell Company, 1910), 35.

Chapter 14 Does God Always Want Us Well?

1. Baxter, *Divine Healing*, 148.

2. Yancey, *Where Is God When It Hurts?* 97.

3. Boggs, *Faith Healing*, 30.

4. Larry Richards and Paul Johnson, *Death and the Caring Community* (Portland: Multnomah, 1980), 39–40.

Chapter 15 Divine Temple or Clay Pot?

1. Claus Westermann, *Genesis 1–11* (Minneapolis: Augsburg, 1984), 265.

2. Ibid., 265–66.

3. T. DeWitt Talmadge, *500 Selected Sermons*, vol. 11 (Grand Rapids: Baker, 1957), 339–40.

4. Richards, *Death and the Caring Community*, 39.

Chapter 16 Praying for the Sick

1. Baxter, *Divine Healing of the Body*, 167.

2. Richards, *Death and the Caring Community*, 38.

3. Curtis Vaughn, *James* (Grand Rapids: Zondervan, 1969), 118.

4. Alfred Plummer, *The Expositor's Bible*, vol. 6 (Grand Rapids: Eerdmans, 1956), 632.

5. Ibid.

6. F. Wilbur Gingrich, *Shorter Lexicon of the Greek New Testament*, 2nd ed. (Chicago: The University of Chicago Press, 1983), 28.

7. Richard Mayhue, *Divine Healing Today* (Chicago: Moody Press, 1983), 111.

8. H. F. Dana and Julius R. Mantey, *A Manual Grammar of the Greek New Testament* (New York: Macmillan, 1955), 137.

9. Rowland V. Bingham, *The Bible and the Body* (London: Marshall, Morgan & Scott, 1939).

10. Vaughn, *James*, 119.

Chapter 17   When God Says No

1. Hans King, *Does God Exist?* (New York: Vintage Books, 1981), 642.
2. Rabbi Harold S. Kushner, *When Bad Things Happen to Good People* (New York: Avon Books, 1981), 134.
3. Ibid., 129.
4. Shirley C. Guthrie, "Human Suffering, Human Liberation and the Sovereignty of God," *Theology Today*, April 1996, 31.
5. Ibid., 32.
6. Sharyn Echols Down, *Prayer, Power, and the Problem of Suffering* (Atlanta: Society of Biblical Literature, 1988), 33.
7. Frank, *At the Will of the Body*, 4.

Chapter 18   "I've Come To Help You Die"

1. Elisabeth Kubler-Ross, *On Death and Dying* (New York: Macmillan, 1969), 36–37.
2. Joseph Bayly, *The Last Thing We Talk About* (Elgin, IL: David C. Cook, 1969), 19.
3. Rabbi Earl Grollman, *Coping with Death and Dying*, ed. John T. Chirban (New York: University Press of America, 1985), 49.
4. Sherwin B. Nuland, *How We Die* (New York: Alfred A. Knopf, 1994), 244.
5. Ibid., 243
6. Richards, *Death and the Caring Community*, 33.
7. Betsy Bunham, *When Your Friend Is Dying* (Grand Rapids: Chosen Books, 1982), 30.
8. Max Lucado, *The Applause of Heaven* (Dallas: Word Publishing, 1990), 189–90.

About the Author

RON DUNN (1936–2001) WAS A graduate of Oklahoma Baptist University and Southwestern Baptist Theological Seminary. He served as pastor to MacArthur Blvd. Baptist Church in Irving, Texas, for nine years, then as Minister-at-Large for that same congregation until his death. He conducted Bible conferences all over the world, was an adjunct professor at New Orleans Seminary, and was an accomplished author. His writings, including *Any Christian Can, When Heaven Is Silent, The Faith Crisis,* and *Surviving Friendly Fire,* have been translated into nineteen languages. He was the founder of LifeStyle Ministries. His wife, Kaye, lives in Flower Mound, Texas, and is now president of LifeStyle. He is survived by two children, Kimberly Kaye and Stephen Mitchell. Ron and Kaye's first child, Ronald Jr., died in 1975 at the age of eighteen.

For more information on LifeStyle Ministries, please contact us at:

LifeStyle Ministries
P. O. Box 153087
Irving, TX 75015
972-570-1570
www.rondunn.com
joannegardner66@comcast.net